WITHDRAWN
UTSA Libraries

RENEWALS 458-4574

DATE DUE

ILL#	8954041	TSC
		JUN 0 2 2000
		NO RENEWALS

PRINTED IN U.S.A.

D1053282

LIBRARIES WITHOUT WALLS 2

the delivery of library services
to distant users

LIBRARIES WITHOUT WALLS 2
the delivery of library services to distant users

Proceedings of a conference held on 17–20 September 1997 at Lesvos, Greece, organized by the Centre for Research in Library and Information Management (CERLIM), Manchester Metropolitan University

EDITED BY
Peter Brophy
Shelagh Fisher
Zoë Clarke

LIBRARY ASSOCIATION PUBLISHING
LONDON

© Peter Brophy, Shelagh Fisher, Zoë Clarke 1998

Published by
Library Association Publishing
7 Ridgmount Street
London WC1E 7AE

Library Association Publishing is wholly owned by The Library Association.

Except as otherwise permitted under the Copyright Designs and Patents Act 1988 this publication may only be reproduced, stored or transmitted in any form or by any means, with the prior permission of the publisher, or, in the case of reprographic reproduction, in accordance with the terms of a licence issued by The Copyright Licensing Agency. Enquiries concerning reproduction outside those terms should be sent to Library Association Publishing, 7 Ridgmount Street, London WC1E 7AE.

First published 1998

British Library Cataloguing in Publication Data
A catalogue record for this book is available from the British Library

ISBN 1-85604-301-0

Typeset in 10/13 Caslon 540 and Zapf Humanist by Library Association Publishing.
Printed and made in Great Britain by Bookcraft (Bath) Ltd, Midsomer Norton, Somerset.

Library
University of Texas
at San Antonie

Contents

ACKNOWLEDGMENTS

There are a number of people whom the editors would like to thank for enabling the publication of this book. Most notable are the staff of CERLIM for their constant support, and in particular Peter Wynne and Geoff Butters who were key figures in the BIBDEL project which led to the establishment of the Libraries Without Walls (LWW) series of conferences. In addition, Geoff Butters' contribution to managing the organization the second Conference was invaluable. A special 'thank-you' is due to Alan MacDougall (Dublin City University), Visiting Professor in CERLIM, a partner in the BIBDEL project team and chairperson at the LWW2 Conference. Grateful thanks are also due to Costas Sophoulis, Ellie Vlachou and Panayiotis Papachiou at the University of the Aegean for their hospitality and their support in managing the LWW2 Conference on the island of Lesvos in Greece.

CONTRIBUTORS

Paul Blackmore, Internet Librarian, Webmaster and Study Centre Librarian, Wirral Metropolitan College, UK

Peter Brophy, Director of the Centre for Research in Library and Information Management, Manchester Metropolitan University, UK

Jan Corthouts, Deputy Director, UIA-Library, University of Antwerp, Belgium

Jenny Craven, Researcher, Centre for Research in Library and Information Management, UK

Denzil Edge, Chair of the Department of Special Education, University of Louisville, USA

Sharon M. Edge, Head of Document Access and Delivery Services, University of Louisville Libraries, USA

Shelagh Fisher, Principal Lecturer and Reader, Department of Information and Communications, Manchester Metropolitan University, UK

Lorraine Hall, Assistant Director, Information Services, University of Sunderland, UK

Joe Hendry, Cumbria County Heritage Services Officer, and President of the UK Library Association (1997)

Sue McKnight, University Librarian, Deakin University, Australia

Maurice Owen, Head of the Fine Art Research Centre, Southampton Institute, UK

Ian Pettman, The Freshwater Biological Association, UK

Richard Philips, Systems Manager, Libraries of the University of Antwerp, Belgium

Kate Stephens, Division of Education, Sheffield University, UK

Julien Van Borm, Director, UIA-Library, University of Antwerp, Belgium

Suzanne Ward, The British Library Document Supply Centre, UK

Alan Watkin, Chief Leisure, Libraries and Culture Officer, Wrexham Borough Council, UK

Peter Wynne, Projects Coordinator, Centre for Research in Library and Information Management, UK

1

INTRODUCTION

Background

'Libraries without walls' as a concept was born out of practical experience. In the early 1990s the rapid expansion of higher education in the UK led to debate about new ways of increasing participation, especially by those who had traditionally missed the opportunity of a university education, for whatever reason. It was recognized that, despite earlier expansion, higher education in the UK remained largely an immediately post-school experience. Furthermore the social mix of university entrants had hardly been altered: higher education remained a middle-class preserve.

Coupled with this situation was a growing realization that the old pattern of a university degree being a qualification for life had gone. The rate of change was such that regular reskilling would be essential to every graduate – the movement which would result in the late 1990s emphasis on lifelong learning was already gathering momentum.

A third issue was the ever more insistent onward march of IT into every area of life. It was clear, even before the World Wide Web had appeared on the scene, that networked information services held much of the future for libraries. Networking implied not only that servers across the world would be used to enable world-wide access, but also that services would be delivered to the desktop. The place of the library would need to be rethought, although only the wilder prognostications of the death of the book posited the possible death of libraries. Be that as it may, the *relevance* of libraries would undoubtedly be a key issue. Would they become the repositories of fading textual artifacts, or could they carve out a niche, or even a key place at the table, in the key institutions of the information society?

Underlying these concerns lay a political agenda in the UK and in Europe which owed much to the traumatic economic events of the late 1980s. It was clear that the USA was the leading economic power in the world. The countries of the Pacific Rim were expanding rapidly and becoming a serious economic force. Could Europe secure its place as the world's third major economic force in the twenty-first century? To achieve this many things would be needed, not least being a secure place at the leading edge of technological achievement. Policies put in place to achieve this ranged from support for Airbus Industrie against the might of the American plane makers, and a massive increase in European funding for research and development. The so-called 'Framework' programmes of the European Commission were put in place to encourage European commercial and other institutions to innovate and bring world-beating products to market. Modest by comparison with the funding programmes for such areas as transport and medicine, there nevertheless emerged a 'Telematics for Libraries' programme, seeking to assist Europe's libraries to lead the world in the application of IT.

It was in this environment that three European university libraries, led by the Centre for Research in Library and Information Management (CERLIM) in the UK, joined forces to research the concept of 'Libraries without walls'. How could university libraries develop so that, using IT in appropriate ways, their services could be delivered to the user? How could the paradigm be turned upside-down: instead of users having to come to the library, the library would come to the users.

Services to distant users

At this time there was, of course, a very considerable body of research and operational experience on which the 'Libraries without walls' concept could be built. In a number of developed countries with populations dispersed over huge geographical areas, such as Australia, Canada and the USA, libraries had been delivering books and other materials by post for generations. This specialist area of library practice had spawned its own biennial international meeting, the Off-Campus Library Services conferences,[1] and these had in turn influenced the production of an extensive bibliography.[2] In general these services were making little use of IT, and indeed the problem of providing access to IT-based systems was only just being addressed. In the UK, the Open University had taken a different approach, using packaged learning materials which minimized the need for additional resources, and urging its students to make their own arrangements with university and public libraries.

A great deal of work had been done over many years to develop our understanding of how users access and use information, but a recent study undertaken by CERLIM at the University of Central Lancashire had shed light on this issue from the off-campus user perspective.[3] 'Franchise' course students (i.e. those studying a University-accredited course delivered by another non-university institution) were compared with on-campus students and their information-seeking behaviour examined in detail through diary studies and focus groups. This provided a sound basis of understanding of user needs on which to develop additional services, which would aim to provide an equivalent level of service for off-campus students to that enjoyed by their on-campus counterparts.

IT developments were beginning to make new services possible. An increasing proportion of the populations in developed countries had their own home computers while even small institutional libraries were being automated. What is more, access to these systems was becoming possible from outside the institutions. In general terms, such developments as the widespread availability of e-mail were starting to make a new approach to communication possible. Online information retrieval was becoming commonplace, with services such as *Chemical abstracts* switching from predominantly paper-based towards online delivery of their information services.

The BIBDEL Project

In 1993 CERLIM coordinated the submission of a proposal to the European Commission's Libraries Programme for a project entitled *Libraries without walls: the delivery of library services to distant users*. The acronym 'BIBDEL' was chosen to link the word 'library' ('bib. . .' In most European languages) with the idea of DELivery. With the acceptance of this proposal, the three library partners, the University of Central Lancashire, Dublin City University and the University of the Aegean began to work together to design, build and deliver experimental services to their dispersed user bases.

Central Lancashire concentrated on the needs of its franchised course students throughout Lancashire and Cumbria. Dublin City chose to deliver to individuals based at home or in a remote office location. In the Aegean the aim was to interlink the small libraries on each of the University's island sites so as to enable users to access the service as a whole.

The Project ran for eighteen months and helped to shed light on many issues which would need to be resolved if such services were to succeed. The results were published in a Final Report.[4] The universities also took the opportunity to make contact with many other librarians and others who were working on or were interested in the topic. As one of the outcomes of BIBDEL, a conference was organized both to present the findings of the Project and to hear of the parallel experiences of others. This was the first Libraries Without Walls conference and was held in Mytilene, Greece where the work of the University of the Aegean could be seen at first hand. The success of this conference led the three universities to agree that an attempt should be made to keep this important issue on the professional agenda through the development of a biennial series. Furthermore it was agreed that in future the conferences should invite papers from experts from around the world, so that through international cooperation all participants would have the opportunity to discuss and debate the issues which surround the delivery of library services beyond physical walls. Thus was Libraries Without Walls 2 born.

Libraries Without Walls 2

The Libraries Without Walls 2 conference, held on the Greek island of Lesvos, 17–20 September 1997, provided an opportunity for researchers, practitioners and others with an interest in this area to discuss the latest developments in the field, and to examine future strategies. In seeking to attract a wider audience to debate these issues, CERLIM is delighted to have secured the publication of the conference proceedings by one of the leading publishers in the field: Library Association Publishing. It is the aim of this volume both to disseminate the papers presented at the conference and to encourage debate and discussion on the issues. The chapters address the principal strategic issues, based on international, regional and sectoral approaches, arising from the provision of library services to distant users.

This state-of-the art collection will enable LIS managers who are seeking innovative approaches to the provision of services to remote users to be fully aware of the latest practice in this important area. It will also assist educational specialists and course developers in increasing their understanding of the role and importance of information in the learning process.

In Chapter 2, Peter Brophy sets out the vision that 'every user, regardless of his or her physical location, should be able to use all library services', and suggests ways to make this vision a reality. The opportunities afforded by IT in the support of distant users, not only in relation to library services but also for teaching purposes, is a theme addressed by several contributors: Denzil Edge and Sharon Edge show how, in their experience at the University of Louisville (USA), building library support for distance learning through collaboration between a teaching department and the library service can deliver high quality distance education (Chapter 3); Paul Blackmore outlines the user, technical and administrative issues of a web-based 'Learning Environment' system (Chapter 4); Maurice Owen discusses 'hyperlinks to reality' and outlines the dangers of a tautological Internet, and the growing need for WWW conceptual indices integrated into library networks (Chapter 5).

Several contributors share their practical experiences in developing services for distant users: Sue McKnight provides an Australian perspective with a discussion of Deakin University's services to off-campus students where library services to distant users have been developing over the last twenty years (Chapter 6); Lorraine Hall describes initiatives for supporting distance learning in Sunderland (UK) (Chapter 7); Julien Van Borm provides an account of the cooperative library network in Antwerp, Belgium (Chapter 8).

Human factors are addressed from a range of perspectives. Jenny Craven and Shelagh Fisher consider the provision of library services for lifelong learners (Chapter 9); Peter Wynne addresses the key human factors in operationalizing services to remote users (Chapter 10); Kate Stephens discusses the library experiences of postgraduate distance learning students (Chapter 11).

Also included in this volume are several papers on work in progress in current research projects addressing the theme of the conference. These include: Alan Watkin on the LISTED and PLAIL projects with a focus on the public library as a local support centre for open and distance learning (Chapter 12); Joe Hendry on the GENESIS Project, with a focus on opening up access to users in remote parts of Cumbria (Chapter 13); Ian Pettman and Suzanne Ward on the EC-funded UNIverse Project which is based on the concept of a virtual union catalogue for libraries (Chapter 14).

The third Libraries Without Walls conference has been provisionally scheduled for September of 1999 and it is hoped that many readers will have the opportunity to contribute to and participate in that event.

References

1 Jacob, Carol J. (compiler), *The seventh off-campus library services conference proceedings, San Diego, California, October 25–27, 1995*, Mount Pleasant, Michigan, Central Michigan University, 1995.

2 Slade, Alexander L., and Kascus, Marie, A., *Library services for off-campus and distance education: the second annotated bibliography*, Englewood, Colarado, USA, Libraries Unlimited, 1996.

3 Goodall, Deborah, and Brophy, Peter, *A comparable experience? Library support for franchised courses in higher education*, British Library Research and Innovation Report 33, Preston, Centre for Research in Library and Information Management, University of Central Lancashire, 1997.

4 Brophy, Peter et al., *Access to campus library and information services by distant users: final report*, Preston, Centre for Research in Library and Information Management, University of Central Lancashire, 1996.

2

LIBRARIES WITHOUT WALLS: FROM VISION TO REALITY

Peter Brophy

Introduction

'Without vision, the people perish' we read in the Bible, and in turbulent times vision becomes ever more important. The enormous changes being forced upon librarians as they seek to harness the possibilities of electronic information without being overwhelmed by its quantity, variety and transience make it imperative that we have a clear vision of the future we are trying to create. As librarians we are forced to ask ourselves whether we are to pursue the technological imperative to its logical conclusion, so aiming to become the masters of cyberspace, or whether the maintenance of collections will provide us with a continued role as the custodians of bibliographic theme parks. Perhaps more likely is a role, as yet ill-defined, in-between combining the power of technology with the enduring legacy of physical recordings of mankind's wisdom and knowledge. Whatever our views, we need to discuss and articulate a vision of how our services can best meet the needs of our users in the future for only by concentrating on the needs of present and future users can any realisable role be built.

The central concern of the Libraries Without Walls 2 conference was, of course, more modest than the development of a grand vision for libraries and information services of all types. The origins of this event lie in discussions held about six years ago in the UK and Ireland, and then with colleagues here in Greece, about the need to find better ways to provide library services to dispersed communities. A joint proposal to the European Commission under its Libraries Programme resulted in the funding of the BIBDEL Project, the subject of Peter Wynne's paper in this volume. Among the closing events of that Project was the first Libraries Without Walls conference, held in Mytiline in 1995. Behind the Project and behind that conference lay a vision which holds as good today as it did in those early discussions. Serving remote and dispersed communities the concern is quite simple. It is that:

**EVERY USER, REGARDLESS OF HIS OR HER PHYSICAL LOCATION,
SHOULD BE ABLE TO USE ALL LIBRARY SERVICES**

What flows from this vision is a quite profound change to the way in which we view libraries. It cannot be right that an individual's access to information should be constrained by accidents of geographic location. Nor can it be right that the educational support of a university library, or the cultural support of a public library, should be constrained by the individual's ability to travel.

Only a few years ago the achievement of true universal access would have been impossible. But technology has given us the opportunity, if it is used wisely, to overcome many of the barriers of distance and to achieve something close to equity of provision. To quote Ann Irving, who was a member of the CERLIM team at the first conference but who has since moved on to a senior position at Thames Valley University near London: 'the concept of a library or information service becomes ever more fluid, moving from a building to be visited when it is open, to a continuous flow of information to be accessed when convenient to the user from any chosen location'.[1]

The question of purpose

This fluidity of concept forces us to ask the questions, 'What is the purpose of libraries?', 'What are libraries for?'. It is extremely important that we develop clarity. The story of the canal company in the north-west of England in the middle of the last century serves to illustrate this point.

The company was operating a canal between two large towns about twenty miles apart. It was very successful, but it was clear that if they were going to build on that success they would have to invest more in the business. So there was a debate among the directors of the company. Half of the directors wanted to buy into the newly-emerging railway companies and develop a rail line between the two towns to supplement the canal. The other half would have nothing to do with such new-fangled nonsense: how could a steam engine possible move the sort of quantities of goods that could be conveyed by canal barge? And anyway, wasn't it accepted good business practice to stay with what you know, to 'stick to the knitting' as modern management gurus would tell us? It came down to the casting vote of the Chairman: he voted to invest in the canal. Plans were drawn up for a three lane dual-carriageway canal. The architects constructed a model showing the outside lanes full of speedboats tailgating, or 'stern-gating', along; the inside lanes were full of massive barges . . . while in the middle lane there was a little old lady wandering around in a rowing boat! Unfortunately before work could begin the company went bankrupt, forced out of business by a new railway company which had stolen all the customers by halving the journey time.

So, why did the canal company go bust? Well partly because they didn't see new technology coming, but mainly because they misunderstood the business they were in. They thought they were in the canal business. They were wrong. They were in the transport business. Canals were the means, not the end.

The purpose of libraries

In the same way we need to be clear about the business we are in. 'What are libraries for?' It is remarkably difficult to find a clear answer to that question. The business we are in is not really running libraries, but more fundamental than that: to say that we are part of the information business is the obvious alternative, but it is even more than that. My tentative conclusion is that the nearest we can come to an answer to the question is to focus on that old triad of:

- data
- information
- knowledge

and to throw in the final key ingredient:

- people.

Data is the raw material which is ordered into information by the application of human minds, and knowledge emerges as information affects the thinking, experience and behaviour of individuals, communities and societies.

However, it is important to go further than a simple definition of the 'stuff' of libraries. We need to take this triad beyond a static statement by recognizing that at the core of libraries and information services there is a dynamic. Libraries and information services deal with the transformation:

- **data** *becomes* **information** *which becomes* **knowledge**

but it also deals with the reverse transformation:

- **knowledge** *becomes* **information** *which becomes* **data**.

Furthermore we need to remember that the transformations of data to information to knowledge and of knowledge to information to data are **social** processes. What is more, the transformation of *data–information–knowledge* does not just transform some 'thing', but inextricably and fundamentally transforms individuals. The *data–information–knowledge* transformation may be seen as the impact of the library on its users today, while the *knowledge–information–data* transformation may be viewed as an impact of the library on society as it stores data ready for transformation into knowledge in the future. In other words our core concern is with changing people's lives: usually in small ways but sometimes quite fundamentally.

To borrow an illustration from a speech which Joe Hendry, the President of the UK Library Association in 1997 and a contributor to this volume, gave at a conference,[2] it is when a child is transformed in very subtle ways by borrowing *Cinderella* from the public library that the 'library' justifies its existence, indeed proves that it is essential to society, or when the research team's work hits the 'eureka' moment as they compare their results with those published by others working at the other side of the world, or when the surgeon changes the procedure he is using in an operation after reading a paper on mortality rates. Library services are ultimately only meaningful in the transformations they engender in people.

But let us not lose sight, also, of the other side of the coin. As a profession we are also concerned with the transformation *knowledge–information–data*. In the past librarians have paid a relatively minor role, concentrating on collection building and cataloguing rather than publishing itself: the process whereby individuals' knowledge is transformed into information and stored as data. But one of the intriguing things about the networked information society is that publication has become an almost trivial process. Unfortunately it is generally assumed that data is not only a free good but also has self-organizing properties, so that the existence of the World Wide Web equates with the realization of the global library and becomes of its own accord, humanity's knowledge bank. What is missing of course is the expertise to organize information and data, and the will to make suitable arrangements for long term storage. We must not lose sight of our responsibilities for this opposite transformation, the capture and making accessible of knowledge, especially as technology is enabling the publication of material much more easily and cheaply than in the past. The expertise of librarians in organizing information is vital, and this may now extend beyond organizing collections of physical objects to involvement in the full publishing chain.

So, to return to my question 'What are libraries for?' I suggest that an answer might be that they are part of a **social** process which transforms stored data into knowledge for the benefit of its users, and knowledge into stored data for the benefit of posterity and that the **benefit** of having libraries can be seen in the **impact** they have on individuals and societies. So when we discuss 'libraries without walls' we are looking at the library as part of the social fabric of its community and we can judge the worth of that library in relation to the impact it has on the people in its community.

The functions of the library

Let us now look at the functions of the library and what the 'libraries without walls' concept implies within an increasingly electronic environment. The traditional library can be thought of as fulfilling six main functions:

- collection acquisition and storage
- cataloguing
- reference and advisory services
- lending, copying etc.
- provision of study space
- preservation and conservation.

The electronic library is somewhat different. There are few theoretical models of the electronic library available though there is a useful EC Report on the subject by Owen and Wiercx.[3] One of the research themes which CERLIM staff have been investigating recently is the exploration of a theoretical model of the electronic library. Figure 1.1 illustrates, from a functional perspective, the elements that make up an electronic library service. It is important to note that such services are *managed* and *holistic*, and as can be seen are far more than a collection of databases or a suite of sophisticated information retrieval software.

However, although this model may describe the electronic library it does not fully articulate the richness and complexity of the real world. For the foreseeable future the book, the journal (at least in its more popular variants), the printed image, packaged audio, packaged video and all the other physical information containers with which we are familiar will be in demand. The challenge, then, is not to replace the traditional library with the electronic library but to find ways to blend the two together to create what is increasingly being called the 'hybrid library'. Again, we do not yet have a good model of the hybrid library. We can, however, make some suggestions as to its functions, noting that it must be more than a traditional library with electronic bits and pieces bolted on: integration will be the key, so that as far as possible users do not need to concern themselves with format or location or access method, but can be supplied with whatever the appropriate content turns out to be.

The hybrid library

Earlier this year I was in the unusual position of being asked to advise a new university on the development of its library services. The University of the Highlands and Islands Project (UHIP) is designed to serve the isolated communities of northern Scotland, including the islands of Orkney and Shetland, the

Access negotiation	Rights to access remote servers
Resource capture and storage	Local fileservers Digitization
Advisory services	Helpdesk Tuition Troubleshooting
Resource discovery	Resource identification Location identification
Resource delivery	Request Acquire Deliver to user
Resource utilization	Exploitation tools
Infrastructure provision	Space Equipment Networks Support services
Resource preservation	Backups Conservation Secure storage
Resource management	Prioritization Value for money

Fig. 1.1 *Model of the electronic library*

Western Isles and small mainland cities like Perth and Inverness and even small-er communities from Argyll in the south to Thurso in the north. The founding institutions are a mix of small colleges offering mainly pre-degree level courses and specialist international research centres: a challenging combination.

The strategic plan for UHIP's Learning Resource Services is based on agree-ment on a series of fundamental principles, which I believe have wider signifi-cance than this single institution in the design of libraries without walls. These principles include:

- close integration between the design and delivery of the curriculum, the information needs of researchers and the organization and provision of learning resources
- the widest possible use of networked electronic information resources, with a presumption that electronic resources will be utilized wherever possible so as to maximize access and availability to dispersed users
- leading-edge library and learning resource services serving as a model for future academic library developments elsewhere
- a distributed delivery model which uses sites as stock holding/access centres
- at each site, a modern, purpose-designed learning centre containing access and enquiry points, study facilities and collections of printed/audio/visual materials in constant use
- distributed expertise and specialist subject collections
- the development of in-depth, archival collections in only a very small, tightly defined number of areas with dependence on other libraries for in-depth collections in most areas
- the right of every student/member of staff to have access to all learning resources, including delivery from other sites and direct delivery for distance learning students
- appropriate administrative systems which enable resource discovery, resource sharing and resource delivery
- systematic monitoring of activity, including each site's contribution to and use of learning resources.

That experience of UHIP, of using technology selectively to build a library without walls from very small beginnings to serve a highly dispersed population is paralleled by other institutions from around the world. This Libraries Without Walls 2 conference included papers which related the experience of building such libraries in Belgium, Ireland, England, the Netherlands, Germany, Wales, Australia and the USA. It is through sharing such experience that we will be able to make the vision a reality, that is:

**EVERY USER, REGARDLESS OF HIS OR HER PHYSICAL LOCATION,
SHOULD BE ABLE TO USE ALL LIBRARY SERVICES**

References

1 Irving, A., 'The context of library and information work worldwide: global realizations', in *Librarianship and information work worldwide*, General ed. M. Line; eds. G. Mackenzie and R. Prytherch, London, Bowker Saur, 1993.

2 Hendry, J., After Dinner Speech: Second International Performance Measurement Conference, August 1997 (Unpublished)

3 Owen, J. S. M. and Wiercx, A., *Knowledge models for networked library services: final report*, Commission of the European Communities (Project PROLIB/KMS 10119), 1996.

3

BUILDING LIBRARY SUPPORT FOR DISTANCE LEARNING THROUGH COLLABORATION

Sharon M. Edge and Denzil Edge

Introduction

Effective distance learning programs require the development and utilization of collaborative partnerships. This chapter describes the collaborative partnership which contributed to the success of the distance education program in the Department of Special Education at the University of Louisville and its impact on the development of a university-wide model for effective library instructional and support services for distance learning. Development of the distance education program and the collaborative partnership with Document Access and Delivery Services in the Ekstrom Library at the University of Louisville is described and the methods used to provide library service to the students are discussed.

The distance education program in the Department of Special Education at the University of Louisville began as a collaborative partnership with Document Access and Delivery Services in the University Libraries, Television Services, Provost's Office, Admission's Office, Bookstore Services, and Information Technology at the University of Louisville. The distance education program was originally supported by the Provost's Office and Information Technology through a collaborative faculty incentive grant for the purpose of exploring new delivery systems for instructional programs. The Department of Special Education and Document Access and Delivery Services in Ekstrom Library were funded through the faculty incentive grant for the purpose of developing a distance education program and providing library services to participants enrolled in the program equitable to those available for on-campus students.

The distance education program

In 1992, the Department of Special Education in collaboration with Information Technology, University Television Services, and the Libraries' Document Access and Delivery Services began offering distance education courses via satellite and interactive television. Currently, the Department of Special Education offers over 22 courses per year via satellite, compressed video and the WWW. This includes a world class program in teacher preparation in the area of visual impairment, leadership courses in special education, and course work in the areas of learning disabilities, behaviour disorders, mental retardation, assertive technology, autism, transition, parent involvement, classroom management, technology and distance learning.

The distance education program in the Department of Special Education at the University of Louisville is committed to delivering progressive teacher preparation programs through advanced technology systems. This award winning distance education program (1994 and 1996 United States Distance Learning Association (USDLA) Telcon Awards) offers high-quality instruction through innovative delivery systems via satellite, compressed video, learning packets, CD technology, and the World Wide Web. Students are taught how to utilize e-mail and electronic library systems to conduct research and download full text of journal articles for literature review and analysis.

The teacher preparation program in the area of visual impairment reaches students throughout the nation and the world. Students are enrolled as a cohort group once a year. They attend a three day Institute at the beginning of the program to learn about distance learning, the WWW, library support, electronic communication and course content. After the Institute, the students spend the following year completing their course work and examinations via distance education.

The Department of Special Education, in collaboration with the University of Louisville's Child Evaluation Centre in the Department of Paediatrics, offers course work to professionals and parents interested in the field of autism. Courses are delivered via interactive and compressed video systems. Parents and professionals use the Kentucky Telelinking Network for consultation and instruction. Also, parents and professionals access information about autism via an electronic library system developed by the Department of Special Education and the Ekstrom Library at the University of Louisville.

The preparation of teacher personnel in the field of special education is changing rapidly, and there is a vast need for qualified special education personnel. In response to this need, the University of Louisville is preparing educators for the twenty-first century via distance learning.

Standards for development of a distance education course and program

In the early days of the distance learning program, standards were developed for the purposes of coordination and cooperation. Through collaboration, the success of the distance learning program was enhanced by the support of numerous units on the University of Louisville campus. This wider support system provided immediate ownership for the program.[1] The entire campus has contributed to the success of the program.

The standards set for program development and support specified that:

- courses would be developed by the Director of Distance Education and the faculty member
- courses would have a producer/director assigned from Television Services (if course delivery is via interactive television) or a webmaster from Information Technology (if the course is a WWW-based course)
- courses would have full library support equitable to that provided for on-campus students
- printed materials developed by the faculty member would be produced by Information Technology Services
- guidelines, course syllabus and program information would be provided via a distance education web page
- printed materials and books for the course would be sold and shipped to the student by next-day air by the University Bookstore
- enrolment assistance would be provided by the Advising Centre in the School of Education, Admissions Office, and the Registrar's Office
- financial support would be provided through a tuition recovery system.

The development of each course begins with the Director of Distance Education meeting with the faculty member to analyse the course content to determine library, television, multimedia, and printing needs. After the content of the course has been compared with program content to determine that certification standards are met, a chart of the particular course needs is developed. A team, consisting of personnel from libraries, television production, multimedia, advising, bookstore services, admissions services and registrar services is assigned to develop the course. Members of this team, coordinated by the distance education program staff begin production. The development of a course normally takes around six months.

Library support for distance learning

The University's first interactive distance education course was offered during the Spring 1993 semester with a full complement of electronic library services. During the Spring of 1992, the University of Louisville announced a Technology

Incentive Grant Program. A faculty member in the Department of Special Education proposed the development of a live, interactive distance education course offered for academic credit via satellite and cable television with students participating interactively in the course via phone and/or computer from their homes or workplaces. Many of the distant students were not expected to be near a major population centre with a library capable of meeting their graduate level research needs. With a philosophy that library research is an essential component of quality education and a belief that distance learning courses should be of equal or superior quality to the same courses offered on campus, two librarians developed a companion proposal designed to provide library service for the School of Education course. Rather than relying on reciprocal borrowing arrangements with other libraries to meet the needs of the University of Louisville's distant students, the librarians proposed offering research support directly from the University library via electronic means. Both proposals were funded and reports were issued upon completion of the projects.[2,3]

The University of Louisville Libraries' library support for distance education program has evolved as the Department of Special Education's distance learning program has expanded and as new programs in other disciplines have been added. The library also, during the 1996–7 academic year, supported graduate-level courses offered via compressed video by the University's Kent School of Social Work and is currently engaged in planning library services for courses in the College of Business and Public Administration and in the Speed School of Engineering. As professors and students have migrated to the Web, librarians have, through electronic library request forms and other information resources available via the Libraries' home page, enhanced the information services available to distant students. Instructing students in information literacy skills needed for distance learning has also become an essential component of the University of Louisville's program of library support for distance learning.

Program of library support for distance education: philosophy

One of the key components of the University of Louisville's program of library support for distance education is the integration of library services into the structure of the course via the professor's WWW home page and any printed course-related materials. A strong belief in the value of information literacy as a necessary component of any educational experience and as an integral element of life-long learning was balanced against the concerns of professors about protecting their valuable class time for discipline-specific course content and the implications of the Report of the National Commission on Time and Learning.[4] Students enrolled in colleges and universities today lead busy lives; they need quick and accurate access to information. Workplace environments are becoming increasingly information-based, and educators must assist students in acquiring the information literacy skills needed to function in those environments.

The collaborative intent of these companion projects was to provide 'one-stop shopping' for the student. The student must, of necessity, communicate with the professor. For many students, communication with the professor via the WWW was a new experience, and they had never accessed either their professor or library services remotely. The collaborators believe that the acquisition of information literacy skills is acquired in steps and that one must be able to crawl before one can walk. Therefore, the University of Louisville system was designed to enable the student to access library services using the same access mechanism used for contacting the professor. This enables the professor to focus valuable class session time on discipline-specific course content without having to allocate separate time for instruction in information literacy skills. The student learns how to access library services by following links on the professor's home page which are linked to the library support for distance education pages. As the students become more information literate through the use of resources accessible via the professor's home page, they are introduced to the broader world of information at their fingertips through links on the Library's pages.

Some of the principles incorporated into the University of Louisville's library support for distance education program are:

- centralization of access
- immediacy of access
- rapid turnaround time for remote delivery
- empowerment of students to access information and to perform their own research on a self-service basis.

Rationale for the development of library service for distance learning

The University's library system is just one of many units that provide support for the School of Education's distance education courses. The technologies that have expanded the delivery of distance education courses and the technologies for providing library resources are converging in ways that argue the need for strong, on-going partnerships between library and distance education programs. The technologies revolutionizing the delivery of distance education courses also are revolutionizing library services. The concept of the 'library without walls' is the logical complement to the 'classroom without walls'. Additionally, 'library service' is considered as an integral aspect of the student's educational experience rather than merely as a 'support' system. This view was summarized by York in 1993:

> Learning depends not only on classroom instruction and dialogue, but also on the student's ability to seek out and critically analyse information . . . Library services are not just another support service; they are a necessary component of any educational experience and an integral part of a lifelong learning process. As distance education degree programs continue to grow and are influenced by technology, planning is essential to meet the information needs of students enrolled in these programs.[5]

Further, the collaborators were convinced that the parent institution receiving tuition payment should bear responsibility for providing support for its distance education programs rather than expecting other libraries in the student's community to assume this responsibility, especially when the materials needed by the student might not be readily available in the community library. The 'Guidelines for extended campus library services' developed by the Association of College and Research Libraries support this belief.[6] The collaborators also believe that, because students engaged in distance learning are paying the same tuition fees as other students of the University, they are entitled to library service which is equitable with that provided to the on-campus community.

Library services provided

Three sets of services are offered: information literacy, reference services, and document delivery services.

Information literacy

Learning depends not only on classroom instruction and dialogue but also on the student's ability to find and analyse information. The ultimate goal of the University of Louisville's library support for distance education program is to enhance students' ability to retrieve information needed for their course work (and for lifelong learning) on a self-service basis and to foster the belief that information literacy is a necessary component of any education experience and an integral element of lifelong learning. The challenge of the University of Louisville's library support for distance education program is to foster library and information literacy among off-campus students engaged in distance learning.

Delivery of information literacy instruction to date has been primarily through one-on-one consultation and an approximately 20-page printed handout inserted in the professor's course notebook which is purchased by all students. The printed handout provides step-by-step instructions (with illustrations of computer screen captures) on how to connect to and use the professor's home page to gain access to library services needed for that particular professor's course. A toll-free phone number and telephone assistance is provided to students who have difficulty connecting or, who, after gaining access still need assistance navigating the pages and using the passwords provided.

For the initial project, library personnel, in conjunction with Instructional Television personnel, developed a short video which focused (in jargon-free language) on ways to identify books and journal articles on a topic and how to get specifically identified books or journal articles. The video quickly became out of date as technology changed; it is being replaced by a multimedia instructional module. This library-initiated, multimedia project developed with technical assistance from personnel in the University's Instructional Quality (IQE) Lab using Macromedia Director and other image, audio, and video software will be linked to the professors' home pages and serve as an introduction to other education resources and information links available via the web. The 'Librarian Assistance' section of the page also includes links to tutorials on how to use the FirstSearch system for searching bibliographic databases and how to use a browser to conduct additional searches for educational resources on the web.

Librarians have also participated in televised instruction via satellite and compressed video. For courses in the School of Education, librarians have both taped video segments in advance and participated in live televised classes interacting with students via phone. In the masters and PhD programs offered via compressed video by the University's Kent School of Social Work, librarians have provided live televised instruction via videoconferencing links and responded to questions from students at the linked sites.

To further the integration of information literacy instruction into distance education programs, the University Libraries submitted a proposal in 1996 for the establishment of a videoconferencing facility in the library. The proposed facility, designed to be staffed and maintained collaboratively with the Office of Information Technology, is intended to serve, until such time as the volume of use indicates a need for a videoconferencing facility within the individual instructional unit, as a site in which instructional faculty can work with librarians and gain hands-on experience to guide decisions about how best to incorporate videoconferencing into their instruction. The videoconferencing facility in the library is also anticipated to serve as a site from which librarians can incorporate both physical library materials available in the building and electronic resources available to students independently of time or place into their instruction.

The Directors of the eight State-Assisted Academic Libraries of Kentucky (SAALCK) are moving toward cooperative resource sharing and implementation of the Digital Library of Kentucky.[7] The proposed videoconferencing site in the University of Louisville Library would allow the SAALCK Library Directors (who also have videoconferencing facilities elsewhere on their campuses) to use personnel resources more effectively. By bringing the expertise of the respective SAALCK staffs together to plan in dispersed work groups, the teleconferencing approach could enhance dialogue and expedite action on several collaborative efforts needed to implement the Digital Library of Kentucky.

The library support for distance education program wants to play a supportive role in those academic units with faculty members who demonstrate interest in integrating library components into their telelearning programs. Through teleconferencing, the library can deliver instruction in methods of remotely accessing information in the University Libraries and from around the world to other sites equipped for videoconferencing.

In summary, the information literacy services provided for students and faculty engaged in distance education include:

- referral to Internet Service Providers (ISPs) in the student's geographical area code
- a 15–20 page printed hand-out for each course which illustrates (with captures of computer screens) the exact steps for accessing the professor's home page and the library resources accessible therein
- instruction to distance students (via television or compressed video or in-person when possible) in online catalogue and Internet usage for retrieval of information
- maintenance of a library-generated World Wide Web (WWW) distance education resource home page with links to other Internet sites relevant to the content of University of Louisville distance education courses.[8]
- provision of tutorials on web use and library research on the web page
- maintenance of a collection of guidebooks and other resources for instruction in use of the Internet for distance learning.

Additionally, the following services are in process:

- development of a brochure outlining the most essential library services for distance education
- replacement of a video-tape on library services for distance students developed in Spring 1993 with a Director multimedia presentation including video clips which illustrate step-by-step procedures for accessing library services for distance education courses.

Reference services

The reference goal of the library support for distance learning program is to enable students at remote locations to identify resources on a topic of their choice. Reference services provided for students and faculty engaged in distance education include:

- provision of access to databases (Library of Congress, National Library of Medicine, and ERIC) for literature searches to determine books and journal articles relevant to course content
- use of databases on a self-service basis by distance students with computer access
- use of databases with assistance of library personnel, occasionally, for any distance students temporarily without access to computers
- availability of a reference librarian via a toll-free number for consultation regarding research strategies.

A Librarian Assistance section is included on the library support for distance education home page. One link associated with the Librarian Assistance page provides the option of sending a question directly to the reference librarian associated with distance education support.

Since most of the courses at present are in the education discipline, emphasis is placed on education resources. In addition to the inclusion of paper fliers on the use of the Educational Resources Information Clearinghouse (ERIC) products and services in paper mailings from the professor or the library, a link is provided to the AskERIC personalized Internet-based service providing education information through the USA and the world. When students submit education-related questions, within two business days they receive a personal e-mail response from one of the network information specialists which includes a lists of citations and Internet resources related to the topic. Links to additional education resources available via the Web are also included under the Librarian Assistance section of the home page.

Document delivery services

The University Libraries' document delivery goal is to make specifically identified library materials available to students in the shortest possible time. The program is designed to enable distance education students to retrieve the full text of material online when possible. When full text is not available online on a self-service basis, the intention of the library support for distance education program is for the University of Louisville Libraries Document Access and Delivery

Services staff to obtain the material from anywhere in the world and deliver it to students in their homes or workplaces.

The document delivery services offered include:

- access via the web-accessible OCLC FirstSearch system to selected databases (including some with full-text journal articles)
- access to required readings placed on course reserve by distance education professors
- electronic provision on a self-service basis for items available in full-text or scanned into machine-readable form
- delivery upon request via fax or mail for items not available in electronic format
- retrieval of books from University of Louisville Libraries' stacks (including charging and delivery of books to students homes via first-class mail)
- retrieval and photocopying of journal articles held in University of Louisville Libraries and delivery of the articles to students via mail or fax
- retrieval of material in micro format held in Ekstrom Library (including digitizing of micro format text for delivery to students to via fax or computer)
- retrieval from other libraries via the OCLC electronic interlibrary loan system of books not held in University of Louisville Libraries for delivery directly to the students/ homes via first-class mail
- retrieval via the Internet (i.e. via the Ariel document delivery system) of journal articles not held at the University of Louisville (including delivery of the articles to students' homes via fax or computer).

There are also additional library services for distance education professors. These are:

- assistance with the development of professors' individual World Wide Web (WWW) home pages (including scanning of professor-generated material into electronic format) (example: <http://www.louisville.edu/edu/edsp/distance/>)
- course reserve (including copyright compliance service for professors)
- hands-on instruction in the Collaborative Learning Centre (an electronic classroom with 25 networked workstations with Internet access, a multimedia instructor's stations, and a state-of-the-art projection system) for professors of distance education courses (and for any of their on-site class sessions upon request)
- access (subsidized by the University Libraries) to UnCover Reveal – an electronic mail alert service which sends, weekly, (a) tables of contents from a list of up to 50 pre-selected journal titles and (b) lists of relevant journal articles

generated as a result of previously established search strategies.

Request forms are available electronically on the Web via the distance education professor's home page. Paper copies of the book and journal request forms which can be used for faxing requests to the library are still included in the professor's course notebook; however, students are encouraged to use the Web forms because, soon, the course notebook will also be made available entirely via the Web. Request forms include notice of copyright compliance and a box to check indicating willingness to pay additional charges above the amount subsidized by the Libraries.

Because University of Louisville distance education students are encouraged to obtain their citations from the world of literature at large using the databases provided, access to the University's online catalogue (Minerva) is not emphasized. Distance education students are not expected to determine ownership of needed items by the libraries of the home institution granting course credit before submitting requests because library personnel are committed to delivering the material even it is not physically present on campus.

Distance education students are told that their library requests should be submitted well in advance of any deadlines because not all items requested will be immediately available on campus. They are told that while some material can be obtained from commercial suppliers within a few days, it may take two to three weeks to obtain material from other libraries and that some material may require more than a month to obtain depending on the source from which it must be acquired. Requests are processed in the order received with no more than five requests processed per day per person. No rush charges are levied because all distance education requests are considered as rush in order to achieve equity of access.

Resources required for library services for distance education

Technology

For database access for distance education students, the librarians initially recommended use of two databases which would cover most of the titles available in North America – the Library of Congress database and the Educational Resources Information Centre (ERIC) database (since the first courses supported were in the School of Education). Web links are now provided to additional databases, including the National Library of Medicine's public database. As stated earlier, the University's own online catalogue was not included because the philosophy was to obtain material needed by distance education students regardless of the location of the material or the student. The student's research should not be constrained by the holdings of a particular library.

Subsequently, OCLC FirstSearch database access was provided, primarily because of access to the full-text of journal articles available in its FastDoc database. The Distance Education Faculty was interested in FirstSearch because it included the Education Index which was viewed as supplemental to ERIC. When it was first implemented as a text-based system, FirstSearch was perceived by the librarians as having an interface which could be used by users with little online search experience or no Web access. The links in several other databases to the OCLC interlibrary loan service and FirstSearch's subsequent Web interface were also attractive features. Originally, FirstSearch was utilized on a per-search basis. However, during Fall 1996, FirstSearch access to a selected set of databases was obtained on a subscription basis through a state-wide consortium agreement.

Electronic course reserve was tested as an alternative for required readings during Summer 1997 utilizing materials already available electronically in full-text. In this model, which was continued in the Fall 1997 Semester, the professor locates articles of interest in the FirstSearch databases and e-mails them to the distance education webmaster. The webmaster links the articles to the distance education professor's home page under the 'Selected Journal Articles for Your Research' section. In the interest of copyright compliance, students are required to enter a user ID and password to ensure access only by students of the University officially registered for the course.

For producing copies of materials held locally in the University of Louisville libraries, the staff use a standard photocopying machine, a scan/fax/copier, and a digital microprinter and fax the digitized document to the user without having to print a paper copy for faxing. For access to material not held locally, the UnCover document delivery service is used as the first choice of commercial vendor because of the ability to fax the document with a 24-hour turnaround time. Material unavailable through UnCover is requested via the OCLC interlibrary loan service with requested delivery via the Internet using the Ariel document transmission system. With the advent of a new University e-mail system, it will be possible to attach documents received via Ariel to e-mail for delivery to distance students electronically.

Staffing

Within the University of Louisville Libraries, there is no separately funded unit or program of library support for distance education. The library support for distance education program has been offered as a collaborative, self-supporting pro-

ject staffed by personnel in Document Access and Delivery Services complemented by the assistance of a reference librarian. Staff and student assistance
wages are recovered from the instructional programs they support. Librarian time
is considered as extended professional development and responsibility – with no
additional compensation. Both of the librarians originally involved in the project
in the Fall of 1992 have continued the job responsibilities they had before becoming involved with distance education. The distance education project was initially undertaken as a professional enrichment and collaborative activity by the two
librarians involved. None of the professional administrative time or librarian time
spent in direct information literacy instruction to distance students is charged
back to the distance education program.

The classified library staff and student assistants who work on the distance
education project are full-time employees of Document Access and Delivery who
work the usual 37.5 hour classified staff work week. The staff and student time
spent on distance education is in addition to the 37.5 hours per week worked for
Document Access and Delivery Services. The individual responsible for
Computer/Network Services in the library support for distance education program works one additional day (7.5 hours) per week at straight time pay for 2.5
hours and at time and a half pay for 5.0 hours. The classified staff person responsible for Document Delivery Services works an additional 2.5 hours per week at
straight time and supervises the approximately 30 hours per week of student
wages charged back to the distance education program. The number of student
hours per week devoted to library support for distance education fluctuates based
on the number of requests received.

Fees charged to students

In the interest of providing equitable service to distance education students, the
same policies regarding fees for library services for students on campus are
applied to distance education students. However, a few exceptions are made in
order to ensure equity of access for distance education students.

The University of Louisville has libraries on both its central Belknap Campus
and on the downtown Health Sciences Campus. Users of libraries on the
University of Louisville's Belknap Campus are expected to retrieve material from
central campus libraries on a self-service basis. However, there is no charge for
the delivery of library material from one campus to users on a different campus.
In order to ensure equity of access for distance education students, no fees are
assessed to distance students for retrieval of material owned in any of the campus libraries, but the labour costs involved in retrieving and copying material for
distance education students are charged back to the academic unit of the respec-

tive distance education program.

For on-campus users, the University of Louisville Libraries pays the first $20.00 of the cost of obtaining material not held in the libraries' collections. Requesters are asked to indicate on the request form any portion of the cost over $20.00 they will pay for an item. Any costs above the $20.00 subsidized by the libraries and agreed to in advance by the requester are automatically billed to the requester's library account. Distance education students are notified of and, upon approval, billed for any charges above $20.00 per item. The $20.00 library subsidy is not charged back to the School of Education distance education program since it is a service offered to all University students.

Assessment

Many higher education accrediting agencies have begun to address the issue of adequacy of library support for academic degree and certificate programs offered electronically via distance education. In the USA., for example, The Southern Association of College and Schools (SACS) Commission on Colleges, in its Criteria for Accreditation, includes a specific section (5.1.7) on Library/Learning Resources for Distance Learning.[9] At the Visions of the Future: Distance Learning for the 21st Century conference, Logan[10] provided some specific questions which should be asked to determine whether an institution is in compliance with the SACS criteria for providing library and other learning resources for distance learning programs. Refinements to the program will be made with these questions in mind.

The original library support for distance learning project described was a spontaneous collaborative effort which developed as the result of a long-standing librarian/instructional faculty relationship; however, the program was firmly grounded on the principles in the American Library Association approved Association of College and Research Libraries (ACRL) *Guidelines for extended campus library services*[11] and in York's *Guide for planning library integration into distance education programs*.[12]

It is important that library personnel know the program needs for distance education initiatives early in the faculty planning process to allow time to plan and budget appropriately for library support for the programs. The University Librarian has taken steps to ensure that library representatives continue to be involved in planning efforts by other academic units for distance education programs in any format. At the University of Louisville, new distance education initiatives and the instructional faculty coordinators assigned to them are communicated by the Provost's Office to the libraries, and library personnel request invitations to give presentations of available resources and services to the faculty coordinators of the programs. Through the University of Louisville Libraries' new Library Liaison Program initiated by the recently appointed University Librarian, librarians also stress the willingness of personnel in the libraries' distance education program to provide appropriate instructional development assistance with webpages for distance education faculty taking care to integrate information resources and offer information support services for faculty and students off-campus at a level similar to those expected by on-campus students and faculty. During the 1996–7 academic year, the library support for distance learning program offered support to the University's Kent School of Social Work for its joint masters and PhD programs offered via compressed video in collaboration with two other Kentucky institutions of higher education. Library personnel at the University of Louisville are also engaged in planning with faculty regarding support for an extended campus program at the USA Army Base at Fort Knox and for various overseas degree programs in Asia, Europe, and South America.

The University of Louisville's accrediting agency criteria state that 'the library and other learning resources must be evaluated regularly and systematically to ensure that they are meeting the needs of their users and are supporting the programs and purpose of the institution'.[13] At the end of each semester since Spring 1993, all students enrolled in distance education courses at the University of Louisville have been surveyed by library personnel regarding the adequacy of services received through the library support for distance education program. The survey has remained essentially the same over the five-year period except for the addition of questions related to enhancement of library services to distant students. Retrospective analysis of both usage data and user feedback regarding the services provided in comparison with the costs involved should supply some interesting conclusions. The results of such an analysis are beyond the scope of this paper but could prove useful in attempts to define and measure the library's effect on educational outcomes, particularly in regard to information literacy competencies gained through library support for distance education programs.

Additionally, the Office of the University Provost at the University of Louisville requires that all academic units conduct an annual 'audit' of service and outreach programs within their respective units in support of accreditation and in anticipation of the outcomes defined within the University's strategic planning document. For the audit of the library support for distance education program information is required on the:

• purpose and consistency with institutional and unit purposes
• activities performed
• funding
• method of evaluation of program activities

- evidence of program effectiveness.

Conclusions

In the USA, the Education Council Act of 1991 (Public Law 102-62) established the National Education Commission on Time and Learning and called for a comprehensive review of the relationship between time and learning in the nation's schools. The Commission's report, *Prisoners of time*, concluded that we in the USA have been asking the impossible of our students – that they learn as much as their foreign peers while spending only half as much time in core academic subjects. Although this report focused on the American public school system, it also states that higher education needs to get involved.[14] The report challenges academic institutions to use technology to transform learning by improving both the effectiveness of existing time and making more time available through self-guided instruction which personalizes learning.

Higher education is trying to cope in an environment of diminished resources, and higher education funding agencies are placing increasing emphasis on improving efficiency in higher education through increased cooperation among colleges and universities. Many states have turned to the concept of distance learning offered electronically through a 'virtual university' as one possible area of cooperation. Colleges and universities are beginning to use telecommunication technologies with increasing frequency to deliver degree programs to students who do not come to their campuses. Higher education institutions have always seemed committed to providing academic support services that students need to complete the work necessary for their degree programs on-campus. Those institutions serving students who do not come to the campus should still be obliged to provide access for off-campus students to the critical services needed for their research and study. Personnel in the University of Louisville's Ekstrom Library have collaborated with the Department of Special Education at the University of Louisville since 1992 to provide students enrolled in its distance learning program with electronic access to information resources.

In October 1996, Kentucky's Commission on Higher Education and Institutional Efficiency and Cooperation proposed the establishment of a Commonwealth University through which existing or new courses at Kentucky's state-assisted institutions of higher education would be offered electronically. The proposal adds that the electronic university should be accompanied by a Kentucky Electronic Library System. The State Assisted Academic Library Council of Kentucky (SAALCK) has already articulated its vision of a digital library network to be carried out in concert with the Kentucky Library Network and the Kentucky Department for Libraries and Archives. Personnel in the University of Louisville Libraries are eager to continue their collaboration with other Kentucky libraries on the development of the proposed Kentucky Electronic Library System.

The University of Louisville Libraries have a five-year partnership with faculty in providing a full range of library services to students enrolled in credit courses and degree programs offered via distance learning. It is exciting to envision a state-wide system which will have as a major part of its mission the support of students and faculty engaged in distance education via both satellite and compressed video and, increasingly, via use of the Internet and World Wide Web as a networked learning environment. Why? Because, it is important to release distance learners from being prisoners of time and assist them in their race to acquire text needed to meet their immediate information and research needs. It is believed that in the process of using a system which integrates library access mechanisms into the professor's home page, students will begin to view library services and information literacy as an integral part of the lifelong learning process.

Those interested in the evolution of the University of Louisville's library support for distance education program, which was first described publicly in a presentation at the American Library Association's 1995 annual conference, can consult the report of the original Instructional Incentive Grant project on the Web at <http://www.louisville.edu/library/ekstrom/dads/about-us/report.html>. In 1996, a teleconference on the project was developed and delivered to the Kentucky Higher Education Computing Conference via satellite. A copy of a videotape of the teleconference is available via interlibrary loan from the University of Louisville's Ekstrom Library. *Bringing us closer* a description of the University of Louisville School of Education's program which the Library program initially supported as its first project, can be found at: <http://www.louisville.edu/edu/edsp/distance/bringing.html>. *Education for the 21st century* at <http://www.louisville.edu/edu/edsp/distance/about-de/> describes how, in order to meet the vast need for qualified special education personnel, the University of Louisville is preparing educators for the twenty-first century via distance learning.

Contacts

University of Louisville School of Education Distance Education Program:
<http://www.louisville.edu/edu/edsp/distance/>
Denzil Edge, Director, Distance Education Program
1-502-852-6421; 1-800-334-8635 extension 6421

University of Louisville Libraries Distance Education Home Page:
<http://www.louisville.edu/library/de-resources/>

Note A packet of information on the University of Louisville's program of library-support for distance education is available upon request. The packet includes: the rationale behind library support for distance education, an overview of the types of support available for distance learning, a detailed listing of the services currently offered to faculty and students involved in distance learning at the University of Louisville, and a sample page from a University distance learning course notebook. A videotape of an interactive teleconference about the University's program of library support for distance learning is also available. Contact: Sharon M. Edge: 1-502-852-8744 or <smedge01@ulkyvm.louisville.edu>.

References

1 Edge, D. (et al.), *University of Louisville Distance Education Informatics and Telematics Institute Business Plan*, Louisville, KY, University of Louisville, 1997.

2 Edge, D. and Hughes, K., *Strategies for classroom management of exceptional children and youth: the University of Louisville's first interactive distance learning course*, Final Project Report and Evaluation, Louisville, KY, University of Louisville School of Education, 1993.

3 Edge, S. M. and Sager, P., *Information resources for distance education: a project report*   <http://www.louisville.edu/library/ekstrom/dads/about-us/report.html> 1993.

4 National Education Commission on Time and Learning, *Prisoners of time*, Washington, DC, US Government Printing Office, 1994.

5 York, V., *A guide for planning library integration into distance education programs*, Boulder, CO, Western Interstate Commission for Higher Education, 1993.

6 Association of College and Research Libraries (ACRL), *Guidelines for extended campus library services*, approved by the American Library Association (ALA) Standards Committee at the 1990 Annual Conference, 1990.

7 State Assisted Academic Library Directors of Kentucky (SAALCK), *Proposal for Kentucky's Virtual University Library*, 1997.
    <http://www.uky.edu/OtherOrgs/SAALCK/saalckvi.html>

8 <http://www.louisville.edu/library/de-resources/>

9 Southern Association of Colleges and Schools, *Criteria for accreditation*, Decatur, GA, 1994, 38, 47, 57.

10 Logan, S., 'Using SACS criteria for evaluating distance learning programs', paper presented at the Visions of the Future: Distance Learning for the 21st Century Conference, Lubbock, TX, 1997.

11 Association of College and Research Libraries (ACRL), *Guidelines for extended campus library services*, approved by the American Library Association (ALA) Standards Committee at the Annual Conference, 1990.
12 York, V., *A guide for planning library integration into distance education programs*, Boulder, CO, Western Interstate Commission for Higher Education, 1993.
13 Southern Association of Colleges and Schools, *Criteria for accreditation*, Decatur, GA, 1994, 38, 47, 57.
14 National Education Commission on Time and Learning, *Prisoners of time*, Washington, DC, US Government Printing Office, 1994.

4

THE LEARNING WEB: A LEARNING ENVIRONMENT FOR REMOTE AND CAMPUS-BASED DISTANCE LEARNERS

Paul Blackmore

Introduction

This chapter examines the initiatives undertaken at Wirral Metropolitan College (UK) to develop an electronic learning environment which delivers teaching and learning resources to learners regardless of time and their location. High quality multimedia and learner support resources are delivered via the Learning Web using the real time interactive functionality of Internet technologies and the multimedia capability of CD-ROM. Multimedia learning materials, self study assessment packages, communication technologies and access to learner support staff are used extensively within the College to provide open and flexible learning for campus based learners. Through the Learning Web these identical learning resources are now also available to the remote learner in the workplace, within the community, at home or from any location that provides access to a multimedia PC and access to the Internet.

The background to the College is discussed, with an overview of the different areas of distance learning provision delivered within the organization and the subsequent need and materialization of a system to provide equal learning opportunities to both campus-based and remote learners. The technology used within the Learning Web is reviewed, indicating the strengths and weaknesses in the delivery of high quality learning materials and the broad aims which the system is designed to achieve. The mechanisms through which these aims are to be achieved are described. The elements of the working model are examined from a user, administrative and technical perspective, and evidence of some of the lessons learnt in the initial trials of the system is included. The flexibility of the system in delivering a wide range of disciplines, which differ significantly in their mode of delivery, is highlighted. A case study is presented using the National Licensee's Certificate endorsed by the British Institute of Innkeeping: this programme is one of the latest and most flexible programmes intended for delivery via the Learning Web. The benefits of using the system over traditional modes of distance learning provision are highlighted. A summary is provided of the components of a theoretical learning framework which the Learning Web aims to emulate. Aspects of the Learning Web are also discussed from the perspective of economical delivery of learning materials in distance and open learning provision. Finally, the future impact which communications technologies may have on the learning environment are also reviewed.

Open and distance learning within the College

Wirral Metropolitan College is one of the largest further education colleges in the UK, with over 20,000 enrolments annually. Educational provision covers all areas of Further Education disciplines and over 60 Higher Education programmes from HNC to MBA level and caters for the training needs of a significant and growing number of small and medium enterprises (SMEs) and corporate clients.

With over 1500 networked workstations spread across 150 locations in Merseyside the College has one of the largest Further Education computer networks in Europe. The workstations provide students, staff and corporate clients access to the Internet, Intranet and a state of the art electronic Learning Environment.[1] A simplified diagram of the College inter-networking of the Intranet and Internet is represented in Figure 4.1.

As with the majority of both further and higher education institutions there is an increasing need for the provision of independent- or student-centred study to be included within the majority of educational programmes at Wirral Metropolitan College. This change within education results in a growing student population becoming increasingly dependent on distance learning resources and support. This concept of distance learning or learners is a broad one but is generally accepted to imply that the learning process takes place away from the traditional learning environment i.e. the classroom and teacher.

In the context of this paper the distance learners may be placed into three categories, namely:

* campus based learners
* corporate site based learners
* remote learners.

Campus based learners

On the whole the campus based learners include those students who are supplementing their tutor led classroom sessions with additional self study within the college library study centres and open access areas.

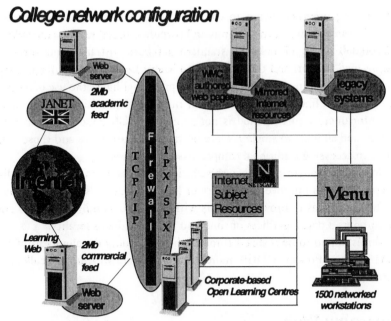

Fig. 4.1   *A simplified diagram of inter-networking of the College Intranet and Internet.*

Corporate site based learners

The College extends its provision further by managing open learning centres located on the sites of major corporates, which include Cadbury's Premier Brands, GM Vauxhall Motors and Lever Brothers. Physically removed from the college campuses, the centres remain connected to the college network via 2Mb megastream proprietary links. This networked provision allows programmes to be delivered on site whilst providing the corporate based learner with open access facilities to the same IT based resources and support available to their campus based counterparts.

Remote learners

The third group may be classed as remote learners, those distance learners studying from home, within SMEs, through third party training providers and those attending programmes in local community centres. Typically these learners may have access to occasional tutor led sessions and possibly the use of a standalone PC.

Once the learners have been grouped into the above categories the inequitable areas of learning provision begin to come to light. With direct access to the College's wide area network, the campus and corporate based learners are able to access £300,000 worth of industry standard software, Intranet and Internet resources, e-mail support and the Customized Menu Learning Resource facility.

This level of equity in the area of learning support highlights the use of megastream links as an effective and economical method of provision for corporate clients. Unfortunately this method is not so economically sound for delivering programmes and support to single remote users, small businesses and those with difficulties in accessing traditional campus based resources.

The College has sought to remove this barrier to access for the majority of distance learners and to improve the quality of learning materials for learners as a whole. The vision was to provide learners with access to learning resources and support 24 hours a day, regardless of time and the individual's locality.

This aim is hoped to be realized through the continuing development of the CD-ROM Internet Project (CDIP), more commonly known within the college as the Learning Web.

The Learning Web

The Learning Web is the name given to Wirral Metropolitan College's electronic learning system which utilizes both Internet and CD-ROM technologies to deliver high quality multimedia learning packages via the World Wide Web and the College's evolving Intranet.

The Learning Web is the result of a project designed to promote teaching and learning at home, in the workplace, on campus and wherever access to the Internet may be gained through a multimedia PC. In recent years many educational and training institutions have used CD-ROM and the Internet to deliver or provide learning support to distance learners. Whilst these technologies have made dramatic improvements to the methods in which distance learning materials are delivered, both still retain inherent weaknesses. The Internet's primary weakness is due to poor bandwidth availability, which drastically reduces the effective and timely delivery of multimedia such as audio, video, high definition graphics and animation.

In comparison, CD-ROMs are capable of delivering over 600Mb of multimedia information in a matter of seconds. However, CD-ROMs have traditionally been used as a 'fire and forget' method of delivering learning materials, whereby the structure of the materials are permanent and the currency of the information can not be readily maintained in a cost effective manner. As with paper based resources there is no indication as to whether the content has been superseded or is outdated. An additional problem remains for the remote user who cannot readily gain access to the interactive learner support which is typically enjoyed by their campus based counterparts. However, using both Internet and CD-ROM technologies in conjunction with one another helps to overcome their respective weaknesses for delivering high quality effective multimedia materials and interactive learner support.

The working model

From the beginning of the project a conscious effort was made to use a non-IT based programme to trial the system. The programme chosen was NVQ level two 'Childcare'. It was hoped that this would highlight the ease with which learners took to the system and might avoid the common criticisms levelled at computer aided learning systems in that the users need to be relatively computer literate to benefit fully from the advantages of such a system. The learning process would initially take place within the campus open access areas.

By their own admission both tutors and staff had very little IT experience, the majority having a moderate knowledge of word-processing and use of a mouse. Comments from both tutors and staff were extremely favourable and acknowledged that the system was easy to navigate and that the quality of the study materials was very impressive. On the whole this was the first time most users had encountered a Web browser and the concept of e-mail.

The system can be viewed from three perspectives: the learner's perspective, and administrative and technical perspectives, as follows.

The learner's perspective

This section provides a brief account of the learner's perspective, or experience, when entering the Learning Web or Web learning environment which is dedicated to their chosen discipline.

Upon receipt of the CD-ROM provided for his or her respective study programme the learner logs onto the Internet, connects to the appropriate login page for his or her chosen programme on the College website and ensures that the CD-ROM is in its drive.

If the learner is accessing the Learning Web on campus via the Intranet the relevant CD-ROM is already loaded on the college network.

If this is the first time the PC has been used to access The Learning Web, helper files check for the presence of a Web browser and whether it is a suitable version for use with multimedia files. The user is then given the option to load a multimedia compatible browser should it be required.

The learner is now presented with the login page which requires the login name and password provided with the CD-ROM or by the learner's tutor. Once logged in, he or she is welcomed by name and invited to select one of three available options:

- start your programme
- enter discussion group
- talk to your tutor.

A detailed description of these options indicates the degree of interactivity and user control:

'Start your programme'

Upon selection of the 'Start your programme' option, the learner is prompted to select the appropriate CD-ROM drive and then presented with the start of the programme. From the contents page the learner may then navigate through the study sections within the programme, which would typically include:

- actual study texts and multimedia materials structured in a manner to guide the learner as the programme dictates
- a self assessment area which includes automated feedback and analysis on results or; forwards the results in a standard proforma via e-mail to the tutor who may then return the results to the learner with constructive feedback
- the Learning Web user guide which provides instruction on using the Learning Web and the recommended methods of using the resources
- frequently asked questions which allow the learner quickly to check those questions, complete with tutor response, which are most commonly asked regarding the programme content and on how to navigate the learning environment.

'Enter discussion group'

The discussion group is an area where learners may talk with their peers or tutors in an open forum. This may be to share information with their fellow learners, discuss programme contents or pose queries to their tutors. At the same time tutors are encouraged to monitor discussions and provide guidance where necessary just as they would in conventional classroom discussions.

Upon entering the discussion group the learner is presented with a list of message headings with the name of the author adjacent to the message. Any responses to the message are listed and indented below.

All the message headings and author names are hyperlinks so the learner may then select one of the existing messages and read through the responses and if required send a reply or start their own thread or topic.

The option is also available to click on any of the names listed and read their background or profile information. If the list is extensive the user may search all of the listed messages within the discussion group using a keyword search facility.

'Talk to your tutor'

The 'Talk to your tutor' facility uses Web form processing to communicate directly with the tutor. This area allows learners to pose questions or discuss matters of confidentiality with their tutors which they may not wish to share with their fellow learners within the discussion area. This facility is also used for submitting assignments: the learner receives a receipt from the Web server detailing the date and time of the transaction.

An administrative perspective

From the beginning of the project, a concerted effort was made to prevent the technology detracting from the learning process. For this reason, all the administration of the user databases is undertaken by the college Web server administrator. The only administration involved on the part of the tutor is the distribution of passwords and login names which again are assigned by the Web server administrator. If mischievous or incorrect messages are sent to the discussion group the tutor may inform the administrator of their presence so that they may then be removed.

The tracking of user activity is also automatically monitored and may be viewed simply by clicking on the profile of the respective user. Printed reports may be requested from the user database detailing all the users on the programme and their activity within the learning environment.

A technical perspective

Once the learner logs into his or her Learning Web programme via the College World Wide Web site, the learning process, structure and delivery of the materials are governed by the Web server from this point forward. The Web server delivers low bandwidth textual information in the form of HTML webpages to the desktop and then seamlessly links to the multimedia material held on the CD-ROM. Learner support is provided by utilizing a combination of interactive Internet technologies, e.g.:

- online conferencing software allows users to discuss study related issues both with their tutors and with fellow learners
- CGI (Common Gateway Interface) scripts held on the Web server permit multiple choice style questioning, assessment and feedback
- using JavaScript, interactive elements may be included to personalize the system, e.g. welcoming users by their first name
- forms processing permits the structured submission of assignments and subsequent feedback from the tutor via e-mail.

Learner tracking is also enabled by a user authentication system which requires users to login to the learning environment of their respective discipline.

The College's Internet connection is further enhanced at the point of login by seamlessly directing campus-based users to resources mirrored on the internal network, the Intranet. In terms of defining the networking paradigm, the system is clearly based on that of a client–server model. Unfortunately, from a holistic perspective, providing a technical definition for the configuration of the Learning Web is not as easy. Claims that the system is solely an Intranet, Extranet or Virtual Private Network (VPN) may be misleading. If anything, each one of these elements can be considered to exist within the learning environment in one form or another.

The programmes

As the number of programmes in the Learning Web portfolio grows, so does the scope of disciplines that are covered. These range from NVQ Childcare to modules in security, safety and loss prevention and a number of foreign languages are currently under development. Ensuring that the technology is used in an effective manner rather than distracting from the content, all material is developed by a combination of educational IT and academic subject specialists working in partnership.

When the project was first conceived it was intended that the initiative would not be designed to replace the tutor nor would it be designed to take the place of the physical classroom. The Learning Web is primarily designed as a learner support facility to provide a value added service to the teaching and learning experience as a whole. The system acts as a supplement to class contact sessions. Equally, for those who may be temporarily housebound through illness or family commitment the system offers a means to access materials and tutor/peer support regardless of time and location. Those with varying work commitments or alternating work-shift patterns are also able to access these resources outside normal teaching hours. Although the system is still primarily designed to enhance the teaching and learning experience rather than to replace the classroom experience, there are certain programmes for which the Learning Web lends itself to the sole purpose of remote distance and open learning.

One example of this is the National Licensee's Certificate (NLC) endorsed by the British Institute of Innkeeping (BII) and other equivalent professional associations. The NLC is available as a qualification for candidates wishing to achieve a recognized standard in Licensing Law. The BII currently delivers two certificates, the NLC On-licence and Off-licence. There are four components to each programme: the syllabuses, the handbooks, the examination and the certificate. At present the Learning Web provides the syllabus and handbook components with additional methods of tutor and peer support. Through recent endorsements this will now include the examination component of the programme allowing all aspects of the course to be studied and assessed remotely.

The benefits of the Learning Web

The value of the Learning Web in being able to offer learning materials 24 hours a day accessible from any location is obviously one of the main advantages such a system has to offer over conventional methods of delivering distance learning provision. This section aims to highlight some of the additional but equally significant benefits gained through the adoption of the Learning Web as a method of delivering networked learning materials to a wide user base.

The HTML format

The hypertext mark-up language (HTML) , the language used to create the webpages within the system, contains many inherent benefits in the effective delivery of information. HTML and its supporting networking protocol hypertext transfer protocol (HTTP) provide an intuitive method of navigating through the learning environment using the easy to use point and click functionality of the Web browser. This user friendly interface provides the learner and tutor with a quick and effective understanding of the technology. HTML requires little or no knowledge of traditional programming languages and allows low cost learning materials to be developed quickly. Exciting multimedia-rich learning materials help to motivate the learner significantly compared with static textual material.

The advent of the World Wide Web and related protocols results from the development of a standardized method to enable electronic documents to be transferred across all computer platforms. The use of webpages therefore allows the same materials to be used and accessed on any internal network which supports a Web browser. These pages may also readily include links allowing the learner to access globally available resources on the Internet. These resources may include electronic journals and academic databases or any other Web/HTML generated resources held on the organization's network.

Allaying fears amongst staff

It is generally accepted that the production and wide availability of a lecturer's teaching materials in electronic form is of great concern and debate. Issues of possible redundancy and plagiarism often surround the electronic delivery of learning materials and such policies are frequently regarded with suspicion from many academic quarters.

During the development of programmes within the Learning Web, dedication and enthusiasm for the project by academic staff has increased as the electronic environment is recognized as an enhancement to the learning process rather than a threat to the traditional role of teachers. This realization is generated by staff becoming aware of the system's dependency on the provision of interactive support, proactive guidance and assessment and that these elements of provision must ultimately be provided by academic staff and programme facilitators. Past research has often argued that interactive support and communication are essential, claiming that their absence will only lead to learners feeling isolated and contributing to their eventual drop out.[2-4]

User tracking

The Learning Web also allows the tracking of learners' online activity. Information that may be monitored on behalf of the tutor includes:

- the date and time of the learner's first login to the learning environment
- the date and time of the of the learner's most recent login
- the total number of connections made by the learner
- the total number of messages posted within the discussion area by the learner.

This combination of monitored parameters helps to highlight problems which the learner may be experiencing. Information indicating a lack of participation within the discussion group or low numbers of connections made to the learning environment help provide the tutor with the opportunity quickly to address the cause of learning difficulties at an early stage. An example of a user profile is given in Figure 4.2.

Monitoring facilities such as this become an essential part of any distance or

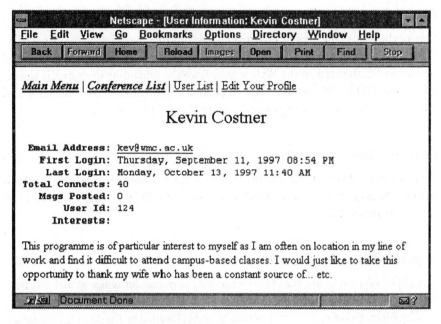

Fig. 4.2 *An example of a user profile highlighting the learner's general interest, e-mail address and user activity whilst accessing the learning environment*

open learning environment especially when it is generally acknowledged that students with poor self-discipline and time management skills require frequent encouragement from their tutors.[5]

Support of legacy formats

The wide functionality of the latest Web browsers has allowed many proprietary file formats to be supported through a single interface. As well as those materials produced in native HTML, proprietary file formats produced by applications such as wordprocessors and spreadsheet packages may also be accessed through the Web browser. This additional functionality of the Web browser has removed the need to republish or convert this material into HTML. Microsoft Word has long been the *de facto* format for the College's learning materials; the continuing availability of plug-ins or file viewers, which are commonly available as freeware, such as Wordview will result in significant cost savings for the College in the future.

Protection of intellectual property

One of the many concerns of institutions distributing materials in electronic format is the theft of the organization's intellectual property. Physical separation of textual media (located on the Web server) from the remaining multimedia (located on the CD-ROM) reduces the likelihood of copying of the College's and author's intellectual property by unauthorized third parties.

Peer and tutor contact

The inclusion of interactive elements within the learning environment helps to remove the feeling of isolation which may have typically been experienced by the remote distance learner.

Improved quality of content

Lecturers who are aware that their work may come under wider global scrutiny, by their own admission feel that this motivates them to apply a self regulatory quality filter, ensuring that the currency and relevance of the learning materials are maintained.

Combined Internet and CD-ROM technology allows high quality multimedia learning materials to be delivered across low band technologies. This combination provides valuable flexibility so that learning materials may be constantly adapted, updated and improved in a timely and cost effective manner. As the page structures and textual information are held on the Web server, updates and additions are made quickly and with ease. The ability for new materials to be received simultaneously by all learners eliminates the costs of reprographics and postage associated with traditional modes of distance learning provision.

Concentrating on the learning process

As the multimedia materials on CD-ROM are in the possession of the remote learner, there is no need to spend lengthy periods of time downloading bandwidth intensive materials. This and the fact that the onus of managing the support software on the College Web server is placed on the technical staff rather than on the learner or tutor, results in more time being dedicated to the study process and further reduces the distraction which may otherwise be caused by the technology.

Conclusion and future developments

This paper has highlighted the continuing developments of an electronic learning environment designed to meet the learning needs of distance learners regardless of their location and the time of use. The combination of CD-ROM and Internet technologies has allowed the College to create a framework for the consistent and effective delivery of a wide range of programmes using multimedia rich learning materials and incorporating a range of learner support facilities.

In researching the design and effectiveness of such electronic learning environments, Sandberg identified several components that need to be integrated within such a system to optimize the learning process.[6] These components were cited as the:

- 'teacher' component, providing guidance and instruction (through teaching staff, intelligent agents or texts)
- 'monitor' component, ensuring that learning takes place (through the tutor, self-discipline of the learner or through a software program)
- 'fellow learners' component, providing peer-contact, enabling group discussion and analysis
- 'learning materials' component, the actual subject content including lesson and task oriented material and problem solving exercises
- 'external information sources', additional materials not necessarily contained within the learning material (e.g. Internet-based resources, handbooks etc.)
- 'tools', any resources in addition to the learning materials which may help facilitate the learning process (e.g. communication software, calculators etc.).

Similarly, Saltzberg and Polyson claimed the need for almost identical components within their 'virtual classroom model'.[7] Throughout this paper examples of such teaching and support components within the Learning Web are clearly evident. However, an additional component is required in the form of a quality check. Monitoring of feedback from both the learner and programme facilitators will ensure that these components will function effectively and may be continually improved.

As the expectancy grows for educational institutions to become increasingly prudent in all areas of financial outlays, so does the need to ensure that learning materials are used cost-effectively. Improvements must include learning materials provision and support becoming more accessible to the learner and available to a wider user base. The Learning Web supports this policy to concentrate on access as opposed to holdings strategies by combining globally available resources, in-house generated materials and outsourced resources, and allowing access to materials by unlimited numbers of learners through both broad and narrow band technologies.

Considerable investment is currently being made into the research and development of broadband solutions to deliver educational materials to remote locations such as the home and work place. Even though this technology has been proven, its sheer cost and the implementation of infrastructure needed mean that this vision is still very much in the future. Despite this reality, any future realization of an information superhighway based on broadband technologies would not suddenly make the Learning Web redundant.

Just as HTML and HTTP will operate across the majority of networking platforms, the flexibility and unique combination of technologies used within the Learning Web will allow the framework to be delivered across multiple telecommunication platforms whether they be broad band or narrow.

Regardless of the technology used and the developments made within the Learning Web the priority will be to continue to improve the learning experience for all users whilst striving for equity in the provision of learning materials for both campus and remote based distance learners.

References

1   Blackmore, P., 'The development of an Intranet within a college of further and higher education', in: *Evaluating the intranet as part of your knowledge management strategy*, Papers from the Aslib conference, Aslib, London September 1996.

2   Garrison,D. R., 'An analysis and evaluation of audio teleconferencing to facilitate education at a distance', *The American journal of distance education*, **4** (3), 1990, 16–23.

3   Jenkins, J., 'New ways of accessing learning', in: *Lifelong learning for the information society*, Papers from the Lilis conference, Genoa, March 1996.

4   Busek, E., 'The role of teachers and trainers in the information society', in: *Lifelong learning for the information society*, Papers from the Lilis conference, Genoa, March 1996.

5   Sherry, L., 'Issues in distance learning', *International journal of distance education*, **1** (4), 1996, 337–65.

6   Sandberg, J. A., 'Educational paradigms: issues and trends', in: *Lessons from learning*, R. Lewis, P. Mendelsohn, eds., Papers from the IFIP TC3/WG3.3 Working Conference, Amsterdam, 1994.

7   Saltzberg, S. and Polyson, S., 'Distributed learning on the World Wide Web', *Syllabus*, **9** (1), 1995, 10–12.

5

HYPERLINKS TO REALITY AND THE KNOWLEDGE MATRIX

Maurice Owen

Introduction

The most important questions facing today's libraries are: 'how will libraries fit into the rapidly developing knowledge matrixes of the twenty-first century?', and 'how will libraries acknowledge and develop strategies which take into account traditional requirements and at the same time plan for future need and potential?'. Given that it is already quite apparent that information and knowledge are rapidly taking on newer and faster means of dissemination, there is also the question of how the library of the future will remain a key part of this evolving process. This chapter is presented from the point of view of the library user and from the perspective of someone involved in the production of knowledge. More specifically the concern here is with library provision for visual forms of communication, such as fine art.

The symbiotic interface between text and image is, historically, a deep one, and certainly as old as the concept of linguistically mediated communication. The concept of the book may have temporarily passed through a pragmatic phase in which this interface became less visible, but this is no longer the case. Imagery, as part of the information/knowledge matrix is clearly very much part of the current agenda for library provision, or if it isn't, it should be. The nineteenth century idea of the public library as the working man's university, was indeed a visionary and egalitarian concept. Mass higher education and libraries linked to pedagogic establishments have done little to dent this original concept. However, there is one development that has made severe inroads into the nineteenth century claim, and it is one that has been driven partly by new technologies. This development is, of course, the ubiquitous Internet and the prospect it offers for 'superhighways' of information and knowledge, all delivered relatively cheaply at the touch of a button, and perhaps even more significantly, in the comfort of one's own home. How will the library of the next century face up to this challenge, and is it indeed an adversarial prospect that confronts it?

The knowledge matrix

To see the Internet as 'adversarial' would be to misunderstand the potential of the information/knowledge matrix and the uniquely different qualities inherent in the various formats through which the user likes to receive data. There is no reason to believe that reading novels on a computer screen would not still continue to be an unpleasant substitute for the much less intrusive book. Conversely, no one wants to waste time and money travelling to a library in search of information which can be more easily gleaned from more immediate sources. Unfortunately there are still many people whose perception of a library is still a place where books are kept and loaned, rather than a key focal point for accessing a wide variety of sources of information and knowledge. Whilst there is no one dominant concept of what a library in the twenty-first century should be, there is never the less the need to reassess its institutional role. Some libraries will no doubt remain, and should remain, highly specialized, providing, for example, an important archival service, or, having as their objective the collecting of highly focused material. Other libraries will try to fulfil a more general requirement. What is, however, common to both types of library is the fundamental need to be visible and accessible from the user's perspective. Much thorough and imaginative work has occurred in recent years in the area of integrated retrieval systems for library based and distant users. Indices and reference catalogues have become increasingly accessible via electronic databases. These are important initiatives. However, the most dynamic retrieval system remains dormant without an enquirer. Any methodology which promotes the spirit of enquiry has to be in everyone's best interest. Questions need to be answered, problems need to be solved, theories need to be tested and ideas need to be encouraged. Everyone can contribute to the information/knowledge matrix. First, however, there needs to be recognition of its existence and second, there needs to be definition, not in an exclusive sense, of what it might consist of.

Different disciplines may well generate unique matrixes. However, it is unlikely that these will remain standalone for long, especially in view of the fact that the very idea of disciplinary exclusivity is increasingly being challenged. Not only is it coming under scrutiny for ideological reasons but also for very pragmatic reasons, since it is becoming increasingly clear that many of the world's problems can only be solved by inter- and multi-disciplinary collaborations. This in itself will automatically lead to the embedding of seemingly standalone matrixes in the macro information/knowledge matrix.

The role of libraries

Before addressing the problem of how libraries could become more proactive in the collection and dissemination of data, consideration should be given to the other possible partners in the chain. Who else can claim to be one of the keepers of the 'sum of human knowledge'? The list of 'knowledge keepers' in Table 5.1 is by no means definitive, nor is it hierarchical, and no doubt every reader will want to add to it, and so they should.

In the twenty-first century how will libraries interface with these key players in the information and knowledge 'industries'? There is also the question of how they will all interface with each other, presuming, of course, that there is some real value in doing so. If indeed educators, information specialists and others are in the business of nurturing the sum of all human knowledge, then this can only be achieved if increasingly holistic approaches to various sources of knowledge, their means of expression and their subsequent repositories are adopted.

In attempting an answer to the above I would like to explore my own discipline's relationship to the wider matrix. As an artist, researcher and teacher in the field of visual art, I am interested to know what the twenty-first century library would offer me and my students, and equally importantly how we can contribute to the concept of the future library. The visual arts are not noted for their communicative immediacy, nor their systematic coherence and therefore if this often unruly and provocative discipline can be constructively brought into the knowledge web, then others, at least in theory, should be less problematical. At present we can tap into the information/knowledge matrix both in reality and via surrogates, in a way not dissimilar to surfing the Internet. Books, via quotes and bibliographies, connect us to other books, which in turn may point us to primary sources, which in turn may lead us to other archives and collections, etc. etc. One can alternatively enter the knowledge web via any one of the above cited contributors to the matrix. Television, radio and newspapers are all equally capable of stimulating the spirit of enquiry, of encouraging us to enter the web. In many ways this is the traditional somewhat chaotic unfocused way in which we engage with knowledge.

Table 5.1 *'Knowledge keepers'*

Museums	Reference catalogues
Galleries	Indexes
Universities	Research centres
Pedagogic establishments in general	Research networks
Archives	Broadcasting: television/tadio
Image banks	Media publications:
Databases	newspapers/journals/magazines
	Websites / search engines / URLs

Formal teaching attempts to provide us with an alternative, a more structured environment in which to assimilate knowledge. To a large extent it does this through an editing process, which it conducts on our behalf. Whilst the editing may or may not be correct it nevertheless provides us with a point of focus which we can either accept, develop, or, reject in favour of some other viewpoint. So what has changed? What has come along to challenge the traditional pedagogic systems? The emergence of electronic technologies in this century has had and is continuing to have a considerable impact on the old knowledge web. The Open University, supported by television and radio, was clearly a pioneer and in more recent years something equally imaginative, although at present far less structured has come along: i.e. the Internet and its World Wide Web of interconnected digital resources. At present it appears to operate as a library without a librarian, and some would argue that this lack of editorial control is a desirable situation.

Knowledge without walls

In considering the knowledge matrix, four key elements may be identified:

- a discipline (e.g. visual art)
- librarianship
- pedagogy
- Internet related technologies.

How can this discipline, or for that matter any discipline, benefit from a collaborative partnership between the other three? All three in their respective ways hold, and seek to disseminate, information and knowledge relating to the discipline, in this instance visual art. Linking the three together would therefore seem to be the logical next step. How can this be achieved? Well, quite simply by providing a discipline-specific integrated guidance system which points to, from and between the collaborative partners. In some circles it is referred to as a subject gateway. Irrespective of the name, the necessity remains the same, which is to develop a coherent point of entry for beginners wishing to access any discipline within the knowledge web. Different disciplines would no doubt wish to create their own appropriate kinds of guidance systems or subject gateways. The possibility of a fully integrated guidance system for visual art is particularly interesting. It would not only open up the enquirer to its various constituent activities such as painting, sculpture, photography, film, video and live art, but would also help to reveal the symbiotic links that exist between them, and equally importantly, associated links with other disciplines. To achieve this the guidance system would have to be appropriately structured.

Visual art is fortunate in the sense that there is a unifying formal/conceptual element which underpins all aspects of the discipline. Visual-narrative in all its various manifestations is the glue which holds the discipline together. It can be seen to be active both in the earliest examples of visual art production and also in the most recent. By distilling out the key concepts which underpin it and by linking these to significant examples, a structured guidance system may begin to emerge. Whilst the system itself would require editorial management and upkeep it could, once placed on the Internet, become reactive as well as proactive. Most significantly of all it could act as yet another catalyst promoting enquiry and thus enter into the knowledge matrix. A system such as this would not only promote distance learning but also encourage library usage. Librarians and particularly subject specialists in libraries would also be in a key position to contribute to its development and management by becoming contributing editors. The guidance system, by existing in a telematic environment would also appear to link seamlessly to other appropriate URLs, which in turn could provide further hyperlinks to any number of resources such as image banks, bibliographies, reference catalogues, indices, virtual museums, galleries and other guidance systems. Additionally, and perhaps most significantly, it would point the enquirer in the direction of primary sources. These may well be held in libraries, or, any number of other locations. In other words the raison d'etre behind the guidance system is not only to further the concept of the library without walls but to embed it into the concept of 'knowledge without walls'.

6

LIBRARY SERVICES TO OFF-CAMPUS STUDENTS: AN AUSTRALIAN PERSPECTIVE

Sue McKnight

Introduction

This chapter describes the Deakin University Library off-campus library service in the context of the Australian higher education environment. In the twenty years that Deakin University has been operating, its library service has earned an international reputation for the innovative and responsive services provided to off-campus students. Advances in information technology have provided tools to extend the library services offered to remote students so that their isolation is being constantly reduced. By focusing on the special needs of off-campus students, the Deakin University Library has been able to improve services to on-campus students and academic staff.

The Australian context

Australia has had a long and distinguished involvement in distance education. Primary school age students who live in the vast outback have been attending the 'School of the Air' for decades. Since the early 1900s the tertiary education sector has been offering university students the chance to complete a degree by studying remotely, in a distance education or off-campus mode. Since the 1970s, however, there has been a stronger emphasis on distance education and, with the globalization of education today, this mode of study is even more important.

Most Australian universities (37 of the 39), are funded by the Australian federal government. As a condition of this funding, universities have to comply with federal government policies as these apply to the tertiary education sector. Two policies are significant in this discussion. Firstly, universities must not charge students for access to resources that are fundamental for their learning, such as access to laboratories, test equipment and chemicals, and libraries. Secondly, specifically with regard to library services, all institutions must aim to provide in their libraries at least 90% of texts and other recommended reading material for a student's course.[1]

The implications for library services to off-campus Australian students are significant. The main impact is that it is the responsibility of the enrolling university to provide the library service (access to at least 90% of texts and recommended reading material). It is not appropriate to expect off-campus students to use the resources of other libraries for their course reading material or to expect other libraries to support university students. Also, libraries cannot charge off-campus students for access to services such as borrowing and reference inquiries as these services are fundamental to their tertiary education and available free of charge to on-campus students.

It is in this context that Deakin University has developed an outstanding reputation for providing tertiary opportunities for students who, for a variety of reasons, do not wish to study in an on-campus mode. In 1995, Deakin University was named 'University of the Year' for its innovative use of information technology to support undergraduate teaching programs. The library was highlighted as an excellent service provider, especially in regard to the services to off-campus students.

Deakin University was created in 1977, as a regional Victorian university based in Geelong, and it has been serving off-campus students since its inception. Today, it has six campuses: three in Melbourne; two in Geelong, and one in Warrnambool. There is 350 km between the furthest campuses and it still retains its strong regional roots despite the strong presence in Melbourne since the merger with Victoria College.

Deakin University off-campus student statistics

In 1996, 13,088 students were enrolled in an off-campus mode of study out of a total student population of 30,191. Off-campus students represent 43% of the student population. 61.5% reside in Victoria, 31.3% reside elsewhere in Australia, and 7.2% reside overseas.

The breakdown of enrolment by Faculty is:

Business and Law	36.3%
Arts	29.1%
Science and Technology	13.0%
Education	12.3%
Health and Behavioural Sciences	7.7%
Cross-institutional enrolments	1.6%

Further, off-campus students are enrolled in the following types of degrees:

Undergraduate (including Honours)   61.2%
Postgraduate coursework   35.4%
Postgraduate research   3.5%

The guiding philosophies of Deakin University Library

All library services are based on three basic philosophies that make Deakin University Library very distinctive because of its strong user focus. The overarching purpose of the library is summed up in its purpose statement: 'We help people learn.'

Another guiding principle is the concept that students have rights. Translated into the library's services, all students, regardless of mode of study, have the right to expect a similar level of library service and support. Therefore, the off-campus library service aims to ensure that remote students have similar opportunities to make reference inquiries, borrow books, obtain journal articles, and undertake independent research as do on-campus students.

The final philosophy, and one under threat as the library is receiving less central funding owing to the Australian Federal Government's policy decision to reduce government funds to universities, is that students should not be 'taxed' for being good library users. This is particularly important for off-campus students who are not charged the direct cost of postage or courier services used to deliver loans of books or photocopies. Off-campus students have enough barriers to tertiary education to overcome without being penalized for being avid readers or diligent students.

Deakin University off-campus library service

Collection development

The cornerstone of any library service is the information resources available to its users. When serving off-campus students, the collection development policy is crucial for providing a quality service. At Deakin University, there is no separately housed collection to service remote learners. Instead the lending collection of all six campus libraries, comprising over 600,000 volumes, is available for loan on request.

The library has developed a formula that is used to calculate the optimum number of multiple copies of a title to be purchased from a unit reading list. The formula takes into consideration whether the unit is taught off-campus and/or on-campus, the number of students enrolled, and the number of other titles on the reading list. Books borrowed by off-campus students stay out on loan for longer periods as the loan length takes into account the delivery time based on whether the student lives in an Australian metropolitan or regional city, elsewhere in Australia, or overseas. It is necessary, therefore, to acquire additional copies of texts and recommended reading resources if the unit is for off-campus delivery so as to ensure that demand, by both on and off-campus students, can be met. The library endeavours to acquire proof copies of recommended reading lists for all units, regardless of delivery mode, to give the maximum time to order titles not already held. Liaison librarians work with the academics in charge of each unit (unit chairs) to ascertain the mode or modes of delivery (on-campus, off-campus, both on and off-campus) and the number of students anticipated each semester.

In addition to this tool for collection development, the library monitors inter-library loan requests to identify titles that should be purchased for the collection. Further, library staff actively encourage research students to make recommendations for purchase.

Information services

An easy to use virtual information service is vital for off-campus students, as they do not have the luxury of being able to go to the reference desk in the library and ask a librarian for assistance. At Deakin University, off-campus students may request subject searches via e-mail, telephone, facsimile and post, and liaison librarians will search the library's catalogue or reference resources such as indexes and abstracting services on behalf of the students. The results of the search are sent back to the student together with either two or three books and/or photocopies that satisfy the information required. If an extensive bibliography were generated by the subject search, then the student would be requested to prioritize the items required and send the bibliography back to the library.

In addition to the above methods, if the student wishes to borrow books or request photocopies of journal articles only, requests can be made via the library's online catalogue system, Innopac, using the 'request an item' function.

Deakin University Library set the benchmark for quality delivery services to off-campus students from its inception. Books are delivered by courier service, express post or, in the case of overseas domiciled students, by airmail. For students living in Australia, a pre-paid return courier or express post satchel is included in the delivery satchel so as to ensure that students can quickly, and at no additional cost, return the items to the library. Overseas students are reimbursed for return airmail postage at the end of each semester.

Anecdotal evidence suggests that one reason why Deakin University attracts off-campus students, particularly higher degree by research students, is the excellent and easy to use off-campus library service. While this may seem an expensive service, in reality it is not. By minimizing the turn-around times for the books, fewer duplicate titles need be purchased. All off-campus students pay an off-campus library levy in their general service fees. This fee, currently A$25.00 per semester for Australian students and A$33.00 per semester for overseas domiciled students, pays the courier and express post costs associated with this service. This is particularly important to ensure that on-campus students are not subsidizing this off-campus delivery service.

The off-campus library levy is much preferable to requiring students to pay per transaction or by the weight of the package dispatched. Such a fee structure would penalize students who read widely. Also, if students were required to pay the return postage costs, the turn around time of books on loan would increase, as the cost would be a disincentive to return the books quickly. In Australia, many other university libraries have now adopted the Deakin University approach of the library providing pre-paid return satchels. It is very popular with the students and is efficient to administer and manage from the library's perspective, as there is minimal paperwork to be processed with each transaction.

Photocopies, which do not have to be returned, are either dispatched with books in courier or express post satchels or sent by regular post. If an item is required urgently, the library will send an article by facsimile. When copyright laws permit university libraries to digitize articles at a reasonable cost, these will be sent via electronic file transfer to the requester's workstation. Already, Deakin University Library uses ARIEL to transmit electronic interlibrary loans of journal articles to requesting libraries. This type of technology can be used to deliver articles to off-campus students as well. There are a number of projects currently underway, e.g. the international JEDDS project, to develop delivery software and management systems to enable digital document delivery to a user's workstation.

Interlibrary loans

Off-campus students may request an interlibrary loan if the item required is not in the library collection. Limits apply to this free service: postgraduate research students may request up to 100 items per year; postgraduate coursework and Honours students can request 25 per year; undergraduate students are supplied interlibrary loans at the discretion of a relevant liaison librarian.

Information services statistics and performance standards

Deakin University Library's off-campus service is the busiest in Australia. Table 6.1 provides a snap-shot of the service.

Table 6.1 *Service statistics*

	1996	To end June 1997
Requests	86,051	44,085
Books sent	54,697	29,822
Photocopies supplied	25,237	12,000
Subject requests	1,929	907
Interlibrary loans	3,226	991

Performance standards are vital in providing an excellent service. The standards given in Table 6.2 apply to the off-campus library service.

Electronic resources

Information technology is seen as a tool for facilitating access to library services. As mentioned before, Deakin University has been honoured for its innovative use of IT. The University has installed extensive local and wide area networks and provides extensive modem banks to facilitate access by remote students to elec-

Table 6.2 *Standards for off-campus library service*

Loans	95% of items held by Deakin University, and available for loan, are dispatched within 24 hours of receipt.
	If a request is received by 11.30 a.m., and the item is available, it is dispatched by 3.00 p.m. on the same day.
	The courier contract requires next day delivery of items to most Australian addresses
Fill rate	90% (actual 92.5% success rate)
Subject requests	85% of subject requests are dispatched within five working days of receipt of request
Photocopies	80% of photocopies are dispatched within five working days of receipt of request

tronic services. Students are also encouraged to open accounts with commercial Internet service providers. In addition, there are 24 hour general-purpose student computing laboratories on each campus and all campus libraries provide electronic information workstations that are available all the hours that the libraries are open.

The library maintains its own Systems Unit and specialized hardware and applications for library services. Off-campus students have 24 hour per day, seven days per week access to a wide variety of electronic services that are also available to on-campus users.

Electronic access to library catalogues is provided. This includes access to the Deakin University Library catalogue, the regional catalogue of all Victorian academic libraries and the State Library of Victoria, catalogues of other Australian university libraries, as well as simple menu access to many catalogues of international libraries.

In addition, off-campus students can gain access to electronic information resources whether mounted locally at Deakin University, remotely located and available by library subscription or publicly available on the Internet. Overall there are some 100 electronic database services available including First Search, CARL Uncover, Current Contents, Project MUSE, IAC Search Bank, ICDL Distance Education Database and so on. Students are issued with the necessary passwords to access subscription database services.

Reciprocal borrowing

In Victoria, a reciprocal borrowing scheme is in place that enables students and staff of any university or any technical and further education college to borrow directly from a participating library. This scheme is based on the philosophy of sharing information resources and providing easy access for staff and students. Net lenders are financially compensated annually by net borrowing libraries. This is a great service for off-campus students who may have easy physical access to another higher education library. In addition, the off-campus library service will provide letters of introduction to other Australian or overseas libraries to facilitate either reading or borrowing access for individual off-campus students. An important part of this service is that Deakin University Library indemnifies its students should they incur fines at a host library. This means the host library is sure of recovering fines should a Deakin University student default and, therefore, more inclined to allow borrowing privileges. It is up to Deakin University Library to recover fines from its delinquent students or staff!

Guides to off-campus library services

Students must be made aware of the library services offered so that they may use these. Therefore, it is necessary to take every opportunity available to provide publicity about the range of services available and access details.

The Deakin University off-campus library service publishes an *Off campus library guide* that is distributed to all off-campus students at the commencement of each yearly enrolment. This guide provides details about the wide range of services available and how to access them, and provides request forms for those without electronic access to the library. Just in case the students do not have electronic access to the library, further request forms are included with each package of books or photocopies sent to a student.

In addition, the *Off-campus library newsletter*, published each semester, is sent to any student who has used the off-campus library service. This form of distribution, of course, only reaches existing library users and does not reach those who have not availed themselves of the off-campus library service. This newsletter gives a more informal insight into the operations of the service and provides handy hints on how best to utilize the library's services.

Search guides are produced for major discipline areas for all students, regardless of mode of study, and provide a brief introduction to the major references resources available from the library.

The library has also produced a 'Research Skills Module' that is available from the library's home page. This module provides useful information, not only about information resources available from the library, but also about referencing styles, bibliography management techniques and the like.

An innovation in 1997 has been personal contact, via a letter from the University Librarian, with every off-campus higher degree by research student, introducing them to their appropriate Faculty Liaison Coordinator. This was initiated after research indicated that this category of student required special library assistance to ensure success with their research.[2] It has proved a successful initiative with many students seeking research advice from the library after receiving the letter.

All of the library's publicity material is available on the library's home page as well as in printed form. The URLs for the *Off campus library guide* and the *Off-campus library newsletter* are, respectively:

<http://www.deakin.edu.au/library/ocserv.html>
<http://www.deakin.edu.au/library/ocnews9701.html>

As well as printed and electronic publicity and instructional material, library staff provide user education classes for off-campus students when they attend residential schools. These classes are at all levels, from basic introduction to library services to in-depth research skills sessions. Many off-campus students are able to visit one of the campus libraries and are welcomed at user education classes held in the library. In addition, if a liaison librarian contacts an off-campus student regarding a subject request, information is provided about why particular reference resources were consulted and why items were selected. This way the student is receiving informal instruction on using library resources in a similar way to on-campus students who are advised at the information desk.

Another avenue for reaching off-campus students has been by participating in student association activities. For instance, in 1997, library staff at the Deakin University Postgraduate Association's annual conference delivered a number of papers and met informally with student delegates to discuss library matters.

Management of the off-campus library service

A special unit within the library manages the off-campus library service. This unit is included within the Resource Delivery Section, which is led by the Resource Delivery Manager who is responsible for loans, inter-campus loans, interlibrary loans as well as the off-campus service.

The Off-Campus Unit is situated at Geelong and is managed by the Document Delivery Librarian. Two library technicians and 4.9 library clerks report to this position. In addition, at each campus library, multi-skilled and multi-tasked clerks retrieve requested items from the shelves and prepare these for daily dispatch to off-campus students. The Off-Campus Unit could be located at any of the Deakin University Library campuses but is housed where the collection is the largest so as to achieve an economy of scale in retrieving items from the shelves for dispatch to off-campus students.

Requests for the off-campus library service are directed to a central location. Telephone and facsimile numbers, for a local call cost from most Australian locations, redirect to the central service. Subject requests are distributed to appropriate liaison librarians at whichever campus they are located. Requests for books and journal articles are forwarded electronically to the holding campus from where the item is dispatched directly to the off-campus student.

As with all library services, there is a close relationship with all other units within the library. Liaison librarians undertake the subject requests; Loans staff at each campus provide services to off-campus students who choose to access the services in person; Systems staff provide the necessary IT infrastructure and support for the automated systems that underpin the off-campus library service; close liaison with Acquisitions and Cataloguing staff is necessary to ensure that items on reading lists are purchased and catalogued. It is indeed a partnership to ensure the service is top class.

Research into library services for off-campus students

Not only has Deakin University been providing an excellent library service for remote students, it has been contributing to the body of knowledge about what library services are required to serve effectively students who choose to study in this mode . A wide range of papers by Deakin University Library staff have been published covering research areas such as:

* who is responsible for library services for off-campus students
* the cost of off-campus library services
* library needs of off-campus higher degree by research students
* library usage by off-campus students.

Future directions

The Deakin University Library off-campus service has an excellent reputation amongst its users and the professional community. However, there is always room for improvement and innovation. During the library's 1997–2000 strategic planning exercise, the following initiatives were identified for implementation.

* To deliver items, in the required format, in the required timeframe, to wherever the user requires. This would involve extending the off-campus style of service to on-campus clients, principally academic staff in the first instance. It is intended to provide a delivery service to staff offices to save academics the time required to come to the library to borrow books.
* To extend the use of IT to deliver services to remote users, for instance using file transfer protocols to send digitized images (copyright permitting) to users who have the appropriate hardware and software to accept files in this way.
* To improve electronic navigation aids; such as providing better access to World Wide Web resources and providing hot links from the library catalogue to owned and leased electronic information resources.
* To extend the existing Electronic Reserve, copyright permissions permitting.
* To link serial titles held physically in the library's collections to titles included in electronic indexing and abstracting services.
* To review the 'information desk' services to extend telephone and electronic services for the benefit of all students.

All of these initiatives will benefit off-campus students as well as on-campus users. While other libraries are coming to terms with the issues to be faced in serving remote users, Deakin University Library is building on its excellent off-campus library services to improve services for the benefit of all library users, whether off campus in Australia or overseas, or on-campus staff and students.

References

1   Higher Education Council, *Library provision in higher education institutions*, Commissioned Report 7, Canberra, National Board of Employment and Training, December 1990, xiv.
2   Macauley, P. and Cavanagh, A. K., 'Information needs of distance education higher degree by research students', *Reading the future: conference proceedings ALIA biennial conference, Melbourne, 6–11 October 1996*, Canberra, ALIA, 1996, 109–18.

7

SUPPORTING DISTANCE LEARNING: EXPERIENCE AND INITIATIVES IN SUNDERLAND, UK

Lorraine Hall

Introduction

The European Year of Lifelong Learning[1] and associated initiatives have challenged traditional ideas about the education and training of the citizens of Europe. The EC definition of 'lifelong learning' emphasizes the importance of broader access to education and the need for infrastructures to support open and distance learning. This and other recent initiatives on lifelong learning have led to a major re-assessment of libraries and information services. Libraries play a crucial role in supporting distributed learning and equip individuals and organizations with the information skills necessary to contribute fully to a knowledge-based society. This chapter describes the initiatives for distributed learning support from the University of Sunderland (UK), examines current issues relating to distributed library services, and considers the challenges and opportunities for the future.

Distributed learning support in Sunderland

A major strategic aim of the University of Sunderland is to support the regeneration of the local economy after the closure of traditional industries such as shipbuilding and coalmining. It also seeks to build partnerships within the region, with further education, with industry and commerce, and with the community. A key aim of the university is to attract learners at all social levels and at all ages, employed or unemployed.

These strategic aims, alongside changes in teaching and learning strategies, have led to an increased emphasis on distance learning. The University of Sunderland's guide to part-time study offers a number of programmes which students can study from a distance. Some may require occasional visits to the university or attendance at a designated study centre and the university is committed to providing high quality support including an appropriate mix of flexible-learning workbooks and contact with a tutor by mail, telephone or at a local study centre. New technology – multimedia, e-mail, video-conferencing and the Internet – is increasingly being used to support distance students.

Impact on learning support services

As a result of these changes to the delivery of the academic programme, the university has reconsidered its traditional library services and now provides:

- more flexible services including a range of delivery methods, different rules as well as new ways of working
- services which students can use independently
- services conducive to different ways and styles of learning
- places to study where users need them (i.e. other libraries, community centres, designated study centres)
- improved access to learning resources
- improved access to printed materials
- access to computer-based materials
- access to the World Wide Web
- interactivity for enquiries and information skills training
- effective library staff training to promote efficient learning support.

Old and new technologies have been used to provide distributed services to offer learning support throughout the City of Sunderland, the north-east of England and, indeed, across the world. The Sunderland initiative aims to target learners at all levels and at all ages in the right places and at the right time. A range of specialist services is provided. At a local and regional level these include the 'Learning City' initiative, collaboration with local public libraries, further education colleges, community colleges and schools, collaboration with local industries, with regional centres of learning, and with hospitals. Specialist services, including Web-based services, for students registered with the university but studying at a distance are also provided. These initiatives and services are described in the remainder of this section.

For distance students registered on university masters courses, for example MBA and MSc students in Hong Kong, Malaysia, and Greece, access to electronic journals via the Web and to bibliographic databases, such as FirstSearch and Blackwells Uncover, is provided. This facility is supported by a faxed document delivery service, which supplies information from the library's own resources and the British Library Document Supply Centre. The university's Information Services Web pages provide all learners with access to library and learning resource services and will eventually provide a common user interface for all the services. At present they include access to information about basic library facilities, information about new services, opening hours, customer service information and feedback, an interlibrary loans template, the online catalogue with access to full-text examination papers and some journal contents pages, electronic journals, hot links to databases in the UK and to subject information gateways, and access to 'self' services of book renewal and reservation.

The University of Sunderland gives full access to the university library's facilities and full borrowing rights for all students in the 15 regional further education colleges which offer university franchised courses. Customized programmes of information skills training are provided to FE library staff and students about e-mail, use of the library catalogue and other electronic services. Network links to the university's online library catalogue are provided to the FE colleges and a support network and an annual seminar at the university for FE librarians has been established. A customized package to members of the Ford & Pennywell Advice Centre, a community college in one of Sunderland's most deprived social areas, includes full access and borrowing rights to library facilities by staff, reference facilities for students, and traditional and electronic information skills training for all Advice Centre members.

A regional centre of learning, 'Learning World', provides HE and FE courses to over a million learners at Europe's largest shopping centre at the Metrocentre in Gateshead. It is a cooperative venture between the University of Sunderland and Gateshead College of Further Education. Courses are delivered to all ages, and range from Saturday morning language courses for children, aromatherapy courses for the local community and shop workers, to part-time MBA courses for businessmen and women. Library services include a print reference collection on site, delivered loans, partnership with Blackwells for book purchase, telephone and e-mail helplines, access to our library catalogue and global networks via the university campus network, and information skills training to all levels of students.

The European Information and Education Centre, based at Jarrow, on Tyneside, provides access to the Internet via the university's campus network and to video-conferencing facilities. Sixth-form students are referred from this service and offered access to University of Sunderland library facilities for reference and information surgeries tailored to their needs. The university has also advised local schools on the development of learning resource centres and access to the Internet. Services to hospital and health trust libraries include access to print collections, advice on collection management, enquiry services and access to some electronic information. Access to all the university's libraries and their reference collections is also provided for local companies. Borrowing rights to textbook collections are guaranteed to subscribers, and customized information skills training for individual companies.

The Learning City (Libraries Access Sunderland Scheme)[2] allows anyone living in Sunderland access to the 29 libraries throughout the city. This includes the 21 public libraries, the four learning centres in the City College of Further Education and the four site libraries in the university. Use of the libraries is for study purposes, and a total of 2,500 study places are now provided for learners. This means that anyone can use the nearest or most convenient library in the city, which is particularly attractive to some of the distance learners. The scheme has opened up access to the university's printed collections for reference purposes. Collaboration with the City Library and Arts Centre has provided 'Learning Places' at two principal public library sites. Access to the Internet and CD-ROM facilities, to word-processing and to information about the academic programmes in the university is provided.

Current issues relating to distributed library services

A number of issues need to be addressed in the provision of effective distance learning support as part of the university's role as a shaper of the information society. These issues include:

- access to services for distance learners
- improved communication with the distance learner
- improved training in information skills and new technologies
- the librarian's role as mediator.

Access to services for distance learners

Research by Unwin[3] has shown that gaining access to library services of a higher education standard is a major problem for those students who live at a distance from their host institution. Although it has been suggested that academics take sole responsibility for providing students with access to relevant supportive literature, academic librarians have always maintained that the ability to use libraries to find information is an essential part of the educational process. This view is supported by the Open University in its student handbook, which states that using libraries is an essential part of education, and that the most important purpose of a university education is to teach students to think for themselves. This implies learning where to find information, and, in particular, how to use the literature of the subject effectively.

Unwin's survey found that the majority of students listed access to books, inter-library loans and journals as their most valued services. In Sunderland, the Libraries Access Sunderland scheme described above broadens access to study places and information collections locally. The Follett Report[4] recommended 69 hours of library opening as a minimum. The University of Sunderland library's extensive opening hours of 83 hours a week during term time ensure that services are available. Electronic access is also very important. A third of students in Unwin's survey used the Joint Academic Network (JANET) to access library information . . . once they knew of its existence and its potential. Experience at Sunderland shows that the international postgraduate students value access to bibliographic databases to locate literature for their dissertations, supported by fast access to relevant documents via fax.

There are at present a number of mutual, reciprocal access schemes most notably those developed amongst the universities in the regions around Newcastle, Manchester (CALIM), and London (M25 Group). Reciprocal access using the host library ticket is not uncommon between university libraries. Some schemes are backed by electronic access and document delivery.

Quality assessment exercises in higher education include learning support as one of the six items that are graded. The *Aide-memoire for assessors when evaluating library and computing services*, published by SCONUL[5] stresses the importance of the availability and relevance of library materials to support all courses, and especially the accessibility of such materials for distance learners.

An effective partnership between academics and librarians is crucial in the provision of appropriate materials. At the University of Sunderland the site librarians are responsible for liaison with their respective Schools, and they attend School management meetings, quality boards, programme and module boards. The Director attends Academic Board and Quality Enhancement Board. One very useful integrating event at Sunderland is the annual Teaching and Learning Conference. Unique among British universities, it gives an opportunity for the whole teaching and learning community to discuss achievements, good practice and trends, and to encourage innovation. It is a very useful opportunity for communication also. Workshops on IT services, information skills training and ways of communicating with the academic community are provided by the Information Services team.

Improved communication with the distance learner

Many libraries are already familiar with 'traditional' ways of communicating with distance learners, such as mail, telephone and fax. Information technology offers a number of ways to improve communication with learners by delivering printed matter, as well as images, sound and video over the network. Network users can find material more easily. A few keyboard searches can find large amounts of information in seconds. Electronic journals offer multimedia capabilities that can facilitate the understanding of complex research. JANET and SuperJANET provide network reliability and common technical standards which provide invaluable access to bibliographic databases and document delivery. The development of MANs (Metropolitan Area Networks) has enabled very high bandwidth, which is being used to access remote information sources, and provides new applications for distance learning and video-conferencing. Increasingly, developments in technology bring the opportunity to bridge distance and bring the library to the desktop of the learner, rapidly accessed through intelligent and easy to use interfaces.

Telematics technologies allow remote users to access enquiry services using a combination of multi-threaded discourse systems and video-conferencing. Opportunities for learners anywhere in the world to see and talk to a librarian at an enquiry desk in the University of Sunderland are closer to becoming a reality. The World Wide Web offers the opportunity for communicating with hundreds of people who share interest in the same topics, for finding information and for searching online catalogues across the world. Universities now offer improved communication by providing electronic access to students' homes, enabling students to be more independent. The university at Sunderland offers a dial-up service called 'Homenet'. Network links provide the means for students to use their e-mail accounts, to contact their tutors and to use more of the library services remotely without going on campus.

Improved training in information skills and new technologies

Some distance learning programmes build library visits into residential time when students visit the campus for face-to-face bibliographic instruction. Teaching and Learning Technology Programme (TLTP) packages have been developed to provide interactive library skills training on anything from a simple literature search to specialist computer information sources. The Information Service at Sunderland is committed to teaching information skills not only to enable students to find and use information for their study, but to enable them to learn and to equip them for the information society. They have developed two open learning initiatives for this purpose: an induction workbook, and an Information Skills module. Networking will provide the means to distribute this courseware to distance learners. The intention at Sunderland is to provide in the near future an information skills training package which will use Internet conferencing technology.

It is also important to recognize that library staff need to update their networked information and teaching skills if they are to provide adequate training for distance learners. The eLib Training and Awareness Programme provides a nationally recognized programme of educational development for library staff which emphasizes the role of librarians in the learning process for students.[6]

The librarian's role as mediator

Librarians are experts in the management and exploitation of knowledge and information. Funds made available as a result of the Follett report[7] in relation to the development of the virtual library have resulted in projects ranging from digitizing text, electronic document delivery, electronic journals, databases and datasets and the development of navigational tools. Collaboration with publishers to address copyright issues, partnerships with academic staff and others have resulted in a 'critical mass' of expertise within the library profession.

Services such as the BUBL information service, and information gateways such as SOSIG, Biz/ed, OMNI and EEVL provide access to quality networked resources available world-wide. Of course, they also act as navigational tools to the bewildering range of information now available, and teaching students how to use them, and how to assess the quality of the information they find, has rapidly become a major part of the librarian's role. JISC and BLR&DD continue to fund projects, such as the MODELS project (MOving to Distributed Environments for Library Services), which will further promote the development of distributed learning support. UKOLN (the UK Office for Library and Information Networking) supports the library community through research and coordination in the areas of networking and bibliographic management.

Barriers

There are barriers to the successful development of services for distance learners; they include:

- Conservative attitudes in academic institutions. This is the attitude which says 'we cannot deliver higher education without a well stocked library'.
- Traditional thinking among users. Mature returners to education, often part-time students, may be afraid to use the new technology. Researchers often cannot find the time to learn how to use electronic sources of information to make life easier for themselves.
- Conventional approaches by library staff. Some librarians are unable to perceive their clientele as anyone other than 18 year old full-time students who are campus-based.
- Difficulties with library collaboration. There is still strong resistance between unequal partners, for example, old and new universities, higher and further education institutions.
- Costs involved. There is a prevailing protective attitude towards resources provided for students of the parent institution.

Conclusions

In summary, distance learners will expect the following services in the future:

- better access to all types of libraries
- flexible services
- remote services
- electronic links.

The belief in Sunderland is that the way forward includes:

- a dual and integrated approach of traditional and electronic delivery services
- the promotion and emphasis of the librarian's role in the learning process in higher education
- the provision of guidance and awareness of the opportunities raised by information networks
- the creation of opportunities for remote access to information.

Sunderland now offers postal and fax delivery of books and documents, and has established telephone and e-mail helplines. The intention is to create an integrated package of networked information which will include a resource bank of digitized text available over the Web, a mediated enquiry service and an information skills package both of which will use Internet conferencing technologies.

Opportunities are available for those not afraid to take them and for those who are willing to investigate the issues which surround seemingly impenetrable barriers. The recent Dearing report[8] recommends closer collaboration in the regions, particularly between FE and HE institutions. It suggested that this be supported by the Funding Bodies and Research Councils. There is also a need to work towards greater cooperation, both in the regions and across sectors...even across industries. Perhaps initiatives like the University for Industry will promote and strengthen partnerships which will benefit all learners, whatever their location. The Committee for Institutional Cooperation, in the USA, which represents the Universities of Chicago, Michigan, Pennsylvania, Indiana, Iowa and others, cooperate on issues such as reciprocal access for libraries, security, risk analysis and special projects. This is despite the fact that in the marketplace, they are in direct competition for students. Solutions must be found to one of the biggest barriers to cooperation: cost. It may be that there are lessons to be learned from colleagues in the USA; it may be that new mechanisms must be worked out at institutional level, in the regions or nationally, if a meaningful way forward for cooperation is to be found.

Events such as the Libraries Without Walls conference offer the opportunity to learn from one other and to eventually work together to solve problems. Whatever happens, if libraries fail to plan strategically for the future, if libraries fail to respond to the challenge, someone else will step in. There is a lot of interest in the computer and media industries in learning, as more people take up learning opportunities throughout life and change careers. As experts in the provision of information and knowledge, librarians cannot afford *not* to meet the challenge.

References

1   Cresson, E., European Year of Lifelong Learning (Presentation), 1996 <http://www.ispo.cec.b>

2   Macdonald, A., 'Sunderland breaks barriers', *Library Association record*, **99** (9), 1997, 459.

3   Unwin, L., 'I'm a real student now: the importance of library access for distance learning students', *Education libraries journal*, **37** (2), 1994, 10–19.

4   Higher Education Funding Council (England), *Joint Funding Councils' Libraries Review Group Report*, Bristol, HEFCE, 1993. (Chair: Sir Brian Follett)

5   SCONUL, *Aide-memoire for assessors when evaluating library and computing services: a SCONUL briefing paper*, London, SCONUL, 1996.

6   Bailey, C., 'Interface: librarians and learning with Jane Core of EduLib', *Ariadne* (8), 1997, 3.

7   Higher Education Funding Council (England), *Joint Funding Councils' Libraries Review Group Report*, Bristol, HEFCE, 1993. (Chair: Sir Brian Follett)

8   National Committee of Inquiry into Higher Education, *Higher education in the learning society*, London, HMSO, 1997. (Chair: Sir Ron Dearing)

8

ANTILOPE, BRONCO, IMPALA AND ZEBRA: ALL ANIMALS RUNNING FOR REGIONAL LIBRARY PROVISION IN THE ANTWERP LIBRARY NETWORK

Julien Van Borm, Jan Corthouts and
Richard Philips

Introduction

The Antwerp zoo is a respectable and world famous institution out of which some animals have been 'borrowed' by the Antwerp regional library network for electronic information and document provision (ANTILOPE, BRONCO, IMPALA and ZEBRA).

This chapter does not deal with theoretical concepts about library provision for distant users. It depicts the settings of the Antwerp regional library network for remote users, who rely on library resources without physically visiting the library or consulting the library staff. These remote users can be users from the other end of the world using the online catalogues of the network, but usually they are members of staff and students of the University of Antwerp, working at home or at their office desk. This user population is going to be extended from 1998 when some database services will be provided to the entire population of the city of Antwerp.

Antwerp cooperative library network

The University of Antwerp (UA) in Belgium was created in 1965 and presently has an enrolment of 10,000 students. All research and teaching disciplines are present with the exception of an engineering faculty. The university is spread over three campuses with several libraries on each campus. This in itself is a good reason for the creation of a system for delivering information to distant users. Moreover, the library automation unit of the University of Antwerp caters for library and information provision in seven other libraries of different types and sizes in the Antwerp region, thus creating a real regional library network extending into the nearby Province of Limburg (University Institution of Limburg) (see Table 8.1).

Table 8.1 *The Antwerp network of research libraries*

	Number of items in the collection	Number of staff	Number of users
University of Antwerp	1,200,000	66	10,000
University Institution of Limburg	70,000	8	1,100
City Library of Antwerp	900,000	30	4,000
Higher education Schools			
• HA	200,000	15	8,000
• HHA	25,000	5	1,000
Special libraries			
• Port Authority of Antwerp	16,000	6	800
• Museum Plantin Moretus	30,000	3	800
Totals	2,441,000	133	25,700

In December 1996 a consortium agreement was signed by the City of Antwerp for the provision of automated library services to the Antwerp public libraries. In the framework of this contract, services and information supply have to start in January 1998. From then onwards research libraries and public libraries will form a 'clump' for library provision to the entire population of the City of Antwerp. The user of the public library will normally start a search in the catalogue of the local public library. If this approach does not deliver the requested information the search will be forwarded automatically to the next levels: the catalogue of all public libraries in Antwerp and the union catalogue of the Flemish public libraries in the northern half of Belgium. If these searches also fail to give the answer a link will be made to the catalogues produced at or maintained by the University of Antwerp: ZEBRA, ANTILOPE and CCB and, licenses permitting, to the CD-ROM databases available through the University of Antwerp (see Figure 8.1).

Virtual library services

The geographical spread of the UA libraries over the City of Antwerp is overcome by a union catalogue for the University of Antwerp (1972), a system of quick interlending of books and photocopied articles (48 h service) and since 1993 by a series of steadily expanding electronic library services. The aim is to make these virtual multimedia library services accessible for every individual member of the cooperating institutions from their library, from their workplace or from their homes via dial-in, X.25, ISDN, Internet, Telenet Flanders or the Metropolitan

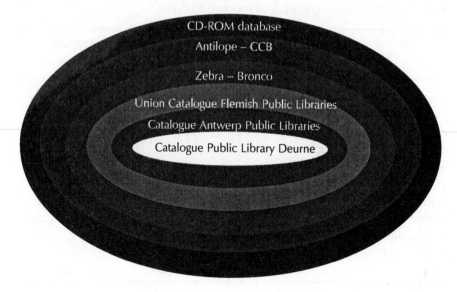

Fig. 8.1 *Electronic library provision for the City of Antwerp*

Area Network of the City of Antwerp. However, copyright rules in general and licensing contracts in particular often put serious restrictions on these intentions.

Presently the main efforts go into the creation of hyperlink integrated services for the end users, starting from a search in one of the available databases right down to the supply of the requested document wherever possible in electronic form for display on and print via a PC. For doing this the UA libraries rely on a series of locally produced or maintained catalogues and a whole set of bought in bibliographies (CD-ROMs often downloaded on the hard disks of a bibliographic server) (see Figure 8.2).

Catalogues

All the catalogues locally produced have been given the name of an animal. It all started with ANTILOPE, a real acronym for what in those days (1973) was a regional union catalogue of periodicals in the Antwerp research libraries (*Antwerpse inventaris van lopende periodieken*). Later on it was decided to continue with this kind of namegiving for other catalogues and related services. All the animals sit nicely on the Web under the shadow of a tree!

ZEBRA stands for Zoeken En BRowsen in de Antwerpse catalogus, or search and browse in the UA catalogue. ZEBRA is the union catalogue of all the libraries

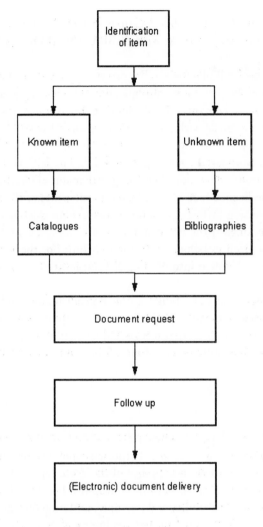

Fig. 8.2 *Integrated electronic library provision at UA*

of the Antwerp regional library network. Presently it includes 1,100,000 book and serial titles with a growth rate of 70,000 items per year, partly the result of an ongoing process of retrospective catalogue conversion in the City Library of Antwerp. The ZEBRA database can be searched freely. For UA users ZEBRA is interlinked with IMPALA, the Belgian electronic document ordering system.

ANTILOPE now stands for ANTwerpse Inventaris van LOpende PEriodieken, or Antwerp union catalogue of periodicals.[1] In 1981 this regional union catalogue became the Belgian union catalogue of periodicals, which includes 173,000 titles with 381,000 locations in 165 libraries. The ANTILOPE database can be searched freely. As with ZEBRA, ANTILOPE is linked into the IMPALA ordering system.

BRONCO stands for Bibliografisch Repertorium van ONline COntents. It is a database containing the electronic contents tables of scientific journals from 1993 onwards. The database contains c.7,000,000 title descriptions from approximately 14,000 scientific journals with a growth rate of over 1,000,000 titles per year. The database is produced by Swets & Zeitlinger in the Netherlands (SwetScan) and is automatically updated every night via FTP. The BRONCO database can only be accessed from workstations belonging to domains of institutions that have contributed to the licence fee. These include participants of the UA library network and libraries using IMPALA, the Belgian electronic document ordering system. UA users working off the campus dial in into the UA central server and by doing so are recognized as belonging to the domain(s) of the UA libraries. The BRONCO database is linked into ANTILOPE for location purposes and further on into IMPALA.

CCB or Catalogue Collectif Belge is the Belgian union catalogue of monographs.[2] It contains all monograph titles from the computerized catalogues of the most important academic and other research libraries in Belgium. The CCB database contains over 4,000,000 records from 28 libraries. The CCB is also linked into IMPALA.

The Web

The Web (WWW), developed as a hypertext and multimedia retrieval system for distributed information, has emerged as the most popular information delivery platform on the Internet. User acceptance of the Web, especially in the academic and research environment, has become widespread because of its interactivity, its multimedia handling capability and its implementation on a global scale. User friendly software like Microsoft Internet Explorer and Netscape Navigator offer high quality browsers to aid navigation. They are available for all platforms and hide the intricacies of the different protocols used.

General benefits of the Web are:

* client–server orientation
* hypertext links in the databases
* integration with the other network resources and services.

Specific benefits for libraries are:

- a user friendly interface (GUI intuitive components like clickable buttons, selection lists, radio buttons and checkboxes)
- full functionality (links to other modules of a library information system)
- no added database complexity (works on top of the online database)
- no learning curve (both novice and expert user of the Web should have no difficulty in mastering the system)
- a real Internet application (it brings the information to the end user regardless of physical location and it also integrates other Internet protocols such as FTP and e-mail for contact with the library's database).

The Web presents library management with the opportunity to implement a unified infrastructure on behalf of its end users. Libraries throughout the world are establishing a presence on the Web by producing home pages, currently the most common active use of the Web by European libraries. These pages include local library information (opening hours, collection and service information, catalogues etc.) but often also provide links to external services (pointers on the Web to other library catalogues, specific subject servers etc.).

The UA libraries opted as early as 1994 for the Web interface as a standard for electronic library information provision to the end users and library staff. The assumption then was that Web use would expand very quickly, especially in the academic world, so that end users very soon would become familiar with the basics, layout and tools of the Web. This assumption proved to be right. Most of the users do not need extra tuition for exploring the UA Web-structured databases. The single home page of the early years has been replaced by a specific home page for end users with an overview of UA library services and another for the library staff. The latter includes manuals, documents, projects papers and also the minutes of meetings. Some of these items are password protected (see Figures 8.3 and 8.4).

All locally produced (ANTILOPE, BRONCO, ZEBRA) or maintained (CCB) catalogues have a common user interface, thus overcoming one of the main problems in electronic information provision: the diversity of the search instruments used (Figure 8.5).

Another problem of electronic information provision is the absence of links between databases of different kinds. This problem has been overcome by interlinking the databases ANTILOPE and BRONCO and by adding an electronic document ordering system (IMPALA) to all of the four databases.

The building blocks in the design of the Web OPAC

The design of the Web OPAC at the UA uses the concept of building blocks,

Fig. 8.3 *Library information provision for end users*

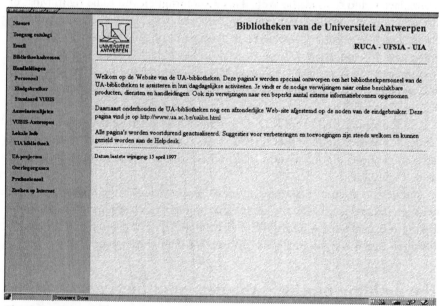

Fig. 8.4 *Library information provision for staff*

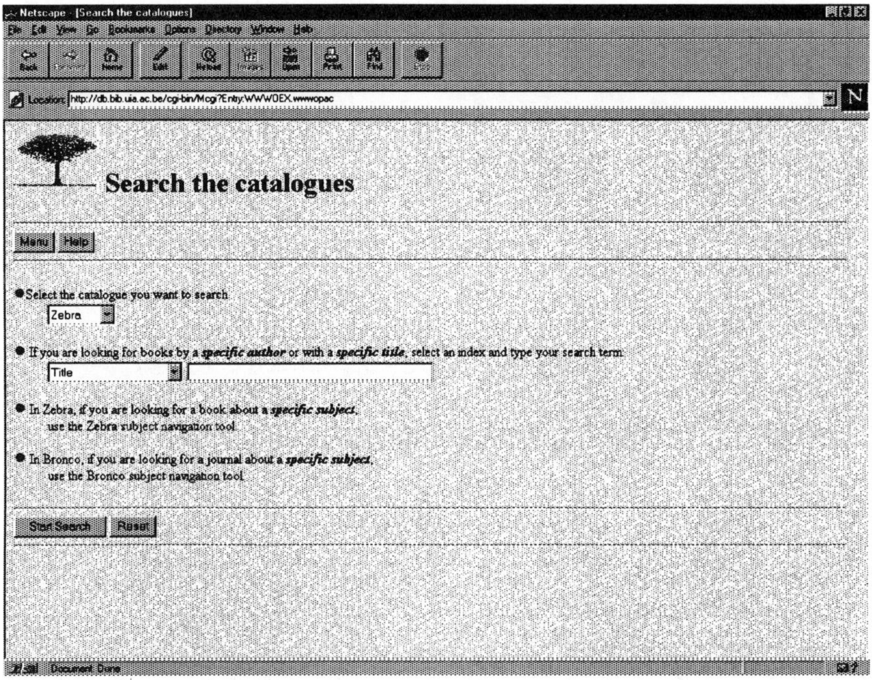

Fig. 8.5 *The search input screen*

being composed of different HTML elements. Designing a user interface through the use of building blocks leads to consistency: the same sequences of actions, names for commands and screen layouts can then be used whenever the user is supposed to undertake similar tasks (see Figure 8.6).

The design is based on the capabilities of the HTML 3.2 specifications. These specifications include the definition of the FORM element and the use of TABLE elements. The FORM element lets the designer create interactive clickable buttons, checkboxes and radio buttons. The main advantages of these buttons are:

- they can be applied in a consistent way
- they improve clarity
- related functions can easily be grouped together
- they allow the user to keep control over the search process.

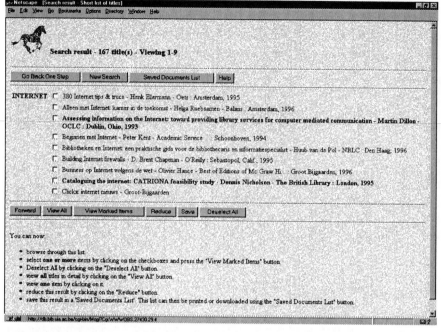

Fig. 8.6 *Typical screen lay out from the Web OPAC at the UA*

Bibliographies

Whereas Belgian catalogues can be produced and maintained locally, thereby using a single end user interface, the same proved to be impossible for the CD-ROM bibliographies. CD-ROM publishers use a wide variety of interfaces. Here also an attempt has been made to create a uniform user interface by relying as much as possible on the Electronic Reference Library (ERL) databases produced by Silverplatter. Moreover the ERL databases are linked with the ANTILOPE database for location purposes and further on into the IMPALA electronic document ordering system for end users. The problem of varying interfaces in the non-ERL databases arises mainly in the human and social sciences, traditionally heavy users of the library resources. It is impossible to create for all these databases a single uniform front end Web interface. The UA libraries, however, will do their utmost in linking some of most heavily used non-ERL databases to the ANTILOPE union catalogue and further on to the IMPALA document ordering system.

Authorization and authentication

Making available electronic information provision outside the library premises requires an authorization system. The UA libraries have set up such a system in the framework of the VIRLIB project, co-funded by the Belgian Ministry for Science Policy in partnership with the Royal Library, the libraries of the Université libre de Bruxelles and IRIS, a private company specializing in the treatment of electronic text and images.[3] In the VIRLIB concept libraries play the role of an intermediary agent in obtaining documents from remote sources for remote users. The VIRLIB project focuses on the development of a user centred system which integrates searching, electronic document ordering and electronic document supply to the end user. As such the VIRLIB project seems to be very much in line with some of the projects in the eLib Programme of the UK. The projects are:[4]

- EDDIS   Electronic Document Delivery: the Integrated Solution
- JEDDS   Joint Electronic Document Delivery Software Project
- LAMDA   London/Manchester Document Delivery

Whenever an end user applies for a document request the ID information supplied by the end user (name and password) is verified against the authentication server (see Figure 8.7).

The main functions of the authentication server are:

- authentication to determine user identification
- authorization to determine whether or not a user is allowed to perform certain actions on certain databases and in the document ordering system
- end user affiliation with a library (users must unambiguously be linked with a library serving as document supply agent).

If the authentication and affiliation are correct the authentication server returns a validation, which gives the user access to the document ordering module, picking up at the same time all user information (name, address, affiliation to department etc.) and all available document information (article title, journal title, location information) (see Figure 8.8).

Once the information on the requested item and on the user is available, the system constructs a URL which is transmitted directly to the Local Request Processing System (LRPS) of the library.

The authentication server will also be accessed when the user requests information on the state of his request (follow up function in the document ordering system). LDAP (Lightweight Directory Access Protocol) technology (X.500

User Administration: 9701

New User Search   Help

● **Global User Information**

Basic Library:	Select form list	UIA

Name: Family Name [PHILIPS]   First Name [RICHARD]   Birthdate [ ]

Identification: Barcode [ ]   OwnId [ ]   Academic bibl [ ]   Password [ ]

Address: Street, Number [ ]   City [ ]   Post Code [ ]

Country [ ]

Contact Info: Email [ ]   Phone [ ]   Fax [ ]

Miscellaneous: Remark [ ]

Message [ ]

● **UIA User Information**

Library ILL services: Ill allowed ☑   paper to home allowed ☑   fax to home allowed ☑   electronic delivery allowed ☑

Renewal Info: Date [10-01-1998]

Local Address: Street, Number [D5]   City [ ]   Post Code [ ]

Country [ ]

Local Contact Info: Phone [ ]   Fax [ ]

Statistics: Usergroup [ATP]

Loan Info: Blocked for loan ? ⦿ No ○ Yes   Loancode [U]

Black List [ ]

Money: In Deposit [1000]   Reserved [800]   Available [200]

Credit codes [77 UY 90; 88 UA 89;]

● **User related functions**

▶ Loan information

▶ User's view of ILL information

▶ SDI information

▶ Accounting information

▶ Academic bibliography

Register Data

Fig. 8.7 *User data for the authentication server*

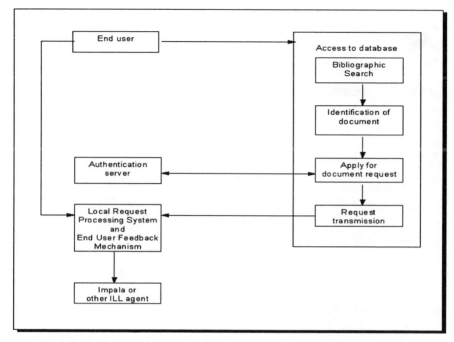

Fig. 8.8 *Place of the authentication server in the document ordering chain*

Lite) will be used in VIRLIB as a common platform for access to authentication servers.

Electronic document ordering

The end user's request for document supply is not sent out automatically. It is routed to the Local Request Processing System of the library to which the end user is affiliated (see Figure 8.9).

After checking, the request is then passed on to IMPALA, the Belgian electronic document ordering system linked into the BLDSC (UK), INIST (France), the libraries of Wageningen, Delft and NIWI in the Netherlands.[5] (See Figure 8.10)

Functions of the Local Request Processing System
Acceptance of incoming requests

The librarian dealing with the incoming request can accept or reject the request. The end user is notified upon acceptance through email and through the follow

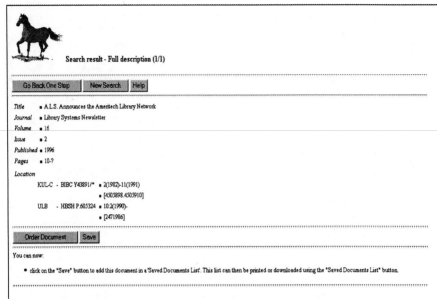

Fig. 8.9 *The order document button*

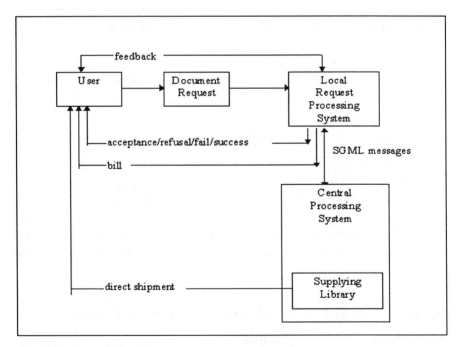

Fig. 8.10 *Request handling*

up facility of the status of his request. Accepted requests are sent to the national IMPALA system using a SGML based protocol.

Refusal of incoming request

The librarian can also decide to refuse the request, e.g. because it contains too little bibliographic information or because the library has a policy not to accept requests that can be fulfilled from the local library collection. The latter is of course irrelevant in the case of distant use. The end user is notified of the refusal via e-mail and through the follow up report of the status of his or her request.

Status information

Document delivery and ILL are often seen as being slow, partly because the process is not transparent. After filling in a document request form the only thing a user can do is patiently wait until the requested item is delivered to his or her desk. The Local Request Processing System has therefore a third and important task: keeping end users aware of what is happening with their requests by transferring the status information of IMPALA to end users via e-mail messages and through the follow up report on the items ordered. These include:

- pending requests (not yet accepted)
- refused requests
- accepted request with status history information
- successful requests (item is supplied)
- failed requests (item cannot be supplied).

Knowing that the end users are looking over their shoulders one might expect a more user centred attitude by the library staff! (Figure 8.11).

Electronic document delivery

When ordering a document the end user has to specify the transmission method. In the case of document supply to distant users this means that a book or journal will have to be delivered to the home or work address, whereas the supply of an electronic journal article can be done via the networks right onto the PC of the end user.

VIRLIB wants to reduce the time span between ordering and actual delivery to the end user by supplying as often as possible an electronic version of the requested article or section of a book (either original full text versions or scanned

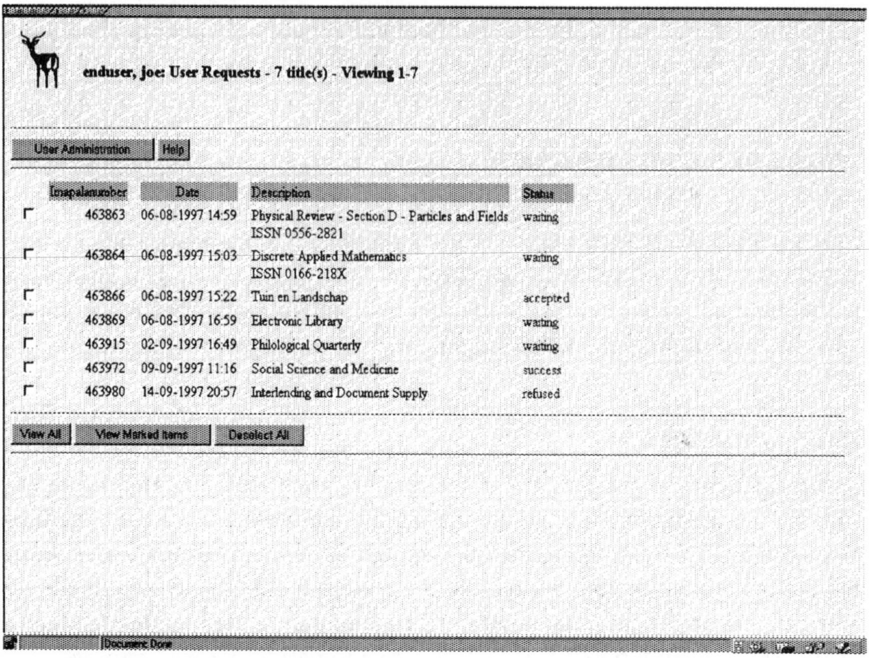

Fig. 8.11 *Status information of IMPALA*

versions of the original text: using PDF documents and TIFF images) right to the desktop of the end user.

TIFF images, PDF documents and Adobe Acrobat Capture have been chosen as the technical components of the document capture system. The well known Ariel software for creating and transmitting ILL documents electronically has been utilized. Ariel has proven to be a highly valuable instrument for transmitting documents between libraries. The electronic document arrives at the requesting library where it is printed and dispatched from there to the end user. However, this is unsuitable in the context of a library without walls, which wants to bring the information directly to the PC of the end user.

Ariel has a number of drawbacks, such as the fact that it does not use the PDF format. The Ariel format, though it contains TIFF images together with a rich set of administrative data, cannot be viewed directly by the end user and is as such not suitable for end user delivery of electronic documents. In contrast to Adobe Capture, Ariel was developed specifically as a library application and it is unlikely that the Ariel clients will be sitting on the workstations of the end users. Ariel should therefore be seen primarily as an alternative transmission method to postal and fax delivery.[6]

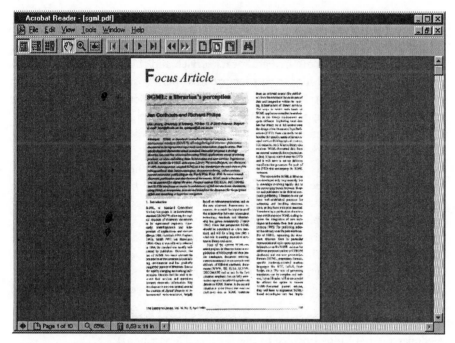

Fig. 8.12 *PDF document in Adobe reader environment*

One of our conclusions was that the Ariel application needs quite a lot of human intervention and relies on a very interactive dialogue. The Association of Research Libraries (ARL) has been aware of these shortcomings and has paid attention to the end user issue whilst developing Ariel version two. But still, in order to view the document the end user needs a TIFF viewer, capable of handling multipage TIFF files. Although these viewers are available, and in the public domain, the TIFF format is not as widely used as PDF and moreover requires a greater degree of user involvement in setting up and integrating these viewers with local e-mail clients.

The solution opted for in VIRLIB has its drawbacks too. Adobe Capture is not easy to use as it stands. Therefore extra tools have been developed that assist libraries in scanning documents and in producing PDF files. This work has been undertaken by IRIS, a Belgian company with an international reputation, specializing in the treatment of electronic text and images. The important thing, however, is that the end user can work with the standard version of the Adobe Reader software (Figure 8.12).

Billing mechanisms

There are two kinds of financial transactions in the process of document delivery: the supplying library has to be paid for its service and the user (or department) may have to be charged for the cost incurred by the library.

The present clearing house concept of IMPALA does not have to undergo major changes. Charging in IMPALA is carried out according to the clearing house principle, a debit and credit system, whereby net requesting libraries are billed quarterly, one single invoice for all Belgian transactions.[7] The Belgian standard cost of an ILL request is 200 BEF (= £ 3.30 at an exchange rate of 60 BEF to £1 sterling). A default value of 200 BEF is built in but can be replaced by the supplying library by any other value e.g. a higher cost for a better product because of instant or speedier supply in electronic form.

If the requesting library wants to recoup the costs incurred by supplying the item to the end user, a billing mechanism (see Figure 8.13) has to be activated. The UA libraries can do this through the administrative information already available in the local server. For every end user the billing mechanism has to indicate the:

* departmental funds (invoice to the Finance Department)

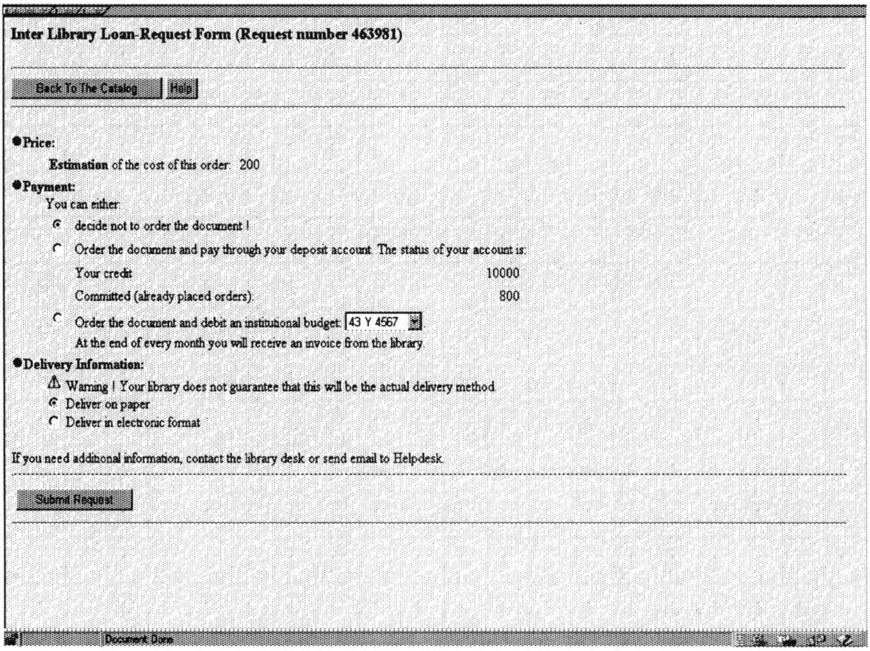

Fig. 8.13 *Billing information*

- project funds (invoice to the Finance Department)
- deposit account (updated in the account server)
- invoice
- expenses covered by the library.

It is up to the various libraries of the University of Antwerp to decide upon the way of recovering the money spent on document delivery.

Problem areas

Copyright

Copyright remains a major obstacle in the provision of electronic documents to the end user and is a serious threat to the VIRLIB project. The Flemish research libraries in Belgium are in the process of establishing a consortium for dealing with commercially available full text documents (Elektron project co-funded by the Flemish Government).[8] It is believed that electronic document supply will only be possible through (and within) a properly established consortium. Scanning of documents still under copyright might be impossible because of far too strict copyright rules, especially in Europe, though IMPALA could easily keep track of copyright fees to be paid directly to the publisher or to a copyright collecting agency by linking the copyright fees to the article information in BRONCO and further on to the journal titles in ANTILOPE.

Help

General information on the UA libraries and their services is available on the libraries' Web sites. Context-related help is available for database searching as well as for document ordering. Ideally, in a Belgian context the information should be provided in three languages: Dutch, English and French. This is not yet the case. Parts are only available in Dutch, others only in English. Apart from these context-related help screens there is a need for direct help to end users on the campus or working at home. It is envisaged that this will be done through a help desk, similar to the one already in use for technical problems encountered by the library staff, with a list of frequently asked questions, e-mail facilities for sending requests for information, a distribution facility for assigning these requests to the library staff, status information on these requests, and a reply facility (Figure 8.14).

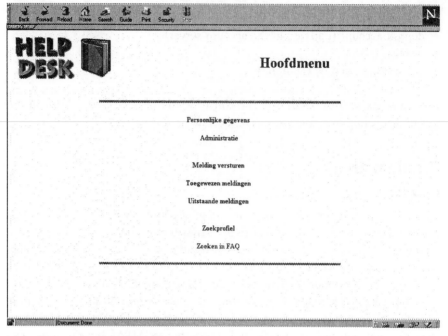

Fig. 8.14 *Help desk for staff members*

Performance measures and indicators

The IMPALA document ordering system has a series of built in performance measures and performance indicators that can be used for performance measurement of the ordering and delivery part of the VIRLIB project.[9] These would have to be enhanced by useful information on the other activities of the electronic library in order to ascertain whether users get what they need, when they need it.

The myths of the Internet

William Miller, president of the Association of Colleges and Research Libraries in the USA has recently published a point of view in *The chronicle of higher education* about the 'troubling myths on the Internet' which might endanger future work in electronic information provision by libraries.[10]

The myths are that:

- all information is now available electronically
- all information is available free somewhere on the World Wide Web, if only one

is clever enough to be able to find it.

These myths suddenly became prominent during the VIRLIB final review meeting in September 1997 when one of the reviewers stated that VIRLIB had no future because all the information required in his discipline could be found instantaneously on the Web.

It is true to say that more and more research disciplines are creating full text document servers, just as they created bibliographies some 20–30 years ago . This can lead to a situation whereby the library profession is losing control over its knowledge base. Examples of this evolution can be found in a series of ongoing projects such as the:

- Physics Eprint Archive (Los Alamos USA)
- European Mathematical Database (coming European funded project)
- Cogprints archive: cognitive sciences (eLib project of the University of Southampton UK)
- Electronic Readings in Management Studies (eLib project Universities of Oxford, Aston and Sheffield, UK).

Whilst in some cases libraries are part of these projects, it is felt that they pose a threat, especially to smaller libraries that constantly see their number of journals shrinking to a level whereby normal research work is hardly possible any more and whereby they become dependent on external sources of information. Organizations will redefine the role of their libraries taking into account the new environment and this might lead to the dismantling of these libraries.

Staff

> Digital libraries require digital librarians . . . Although the broad requirements of digital libraries may be the same as with non-digital collections, any similarity ends there . . . Present day digital librarians find themselves doing almost nothing they learned in graduate school and very little that is familiar. Furthermore the technology is advancing at such a rapid pace that what is learned today will be soon outdated. Therefore it is more important that digital librarians possess particular personal qualities (which are innate) rather than specific technical expertise (which can be learned).

The above is a statement by K. Hastings and R. Tennant.[11] If this statement is true, and at least partly it is, almost none of the present day librarians of the

University of Antwerp would be able to function in our libraries, or in the future hybrid libraries: printed books and periodicals alongside electronic information.

The IMPEL 1 project conducted in 1993–5 by the University of Northumbria at Newcastle (UK) has investigated the social, organizational and cultural impacts on academic library staff working in an increasingly electronic environment.[12] It was followed by the IMPEL 2 project, part of the UK Electronic Libraries Programme (eLib).[13] Findings from the IMPEL projects were that for library and information staff working in an increasingly electronic environment has had an impact on:

- workload
- job satisfaction
- effectiveness
- technical expertise
- group dynamics.

Since then more studies of this kind have been conducted in the USA and in Europe confirming the findings of the IMPEL studies and adding one more: deprofessionalization, the library profession losing control over its knowledge databases.[14]

In the Antwerp libraries many of the staff were hired before any form of library automation began to change the librarian's job. Most started their library career at a time when the term automated library meant a library having an automated library catalogue. Only recently have a few members of staff been recruited to deal with electronic library provision in a hybrid library. Hence there is a huge problem of retraining the staff. A programme has been launched that deals with:

- general information provision on the libraries policy towards electronic information provision
- training and retraining in basic PC functions
- training and retraining in the use of the local catalogues
- training and retraining in the use of CD-ROM bibliographies
- future training in scanning and electronic document provision.

In spite of all this awareness raising and training, at least 10% of the University of Antwerp library staff experience serious difficulties in acquiring new skills.[15] Seeing something done does not equal being able to do it yourself, especially when a variety of skills have to be combined for effective user service. In some cases early retirement under financially and socially acceptable conditions offers a solution. For other members of staff the problem not only remains but may grow as pressure on the libraries builds up.

Many members of staff find it difficult to work in an ever changing environment. This is in contrast to the past when work in a library was seen as the quietest job on earth. The reality of today is a library under pressure, in continuous transformation, integrating old and new into a hybrid library structure, trying to give access to all learning resources for every member of the community it has to serve and therefore requiring enthusiastic librarians.

References

1   <http://www.ua.ac.be/MAN/ANTILOPEE/>
2   <http://www.libis.kuleuven.ac.be/libis/ccb/index.html>
3   <http://www.ua.ac.be/VIRLIB>
4   <http://ukoln.bath.ac.uk/elib>
5   Van Borm, J., 'Impala, le système belge de commande électronique de documents', *Lectures*, **88**, 1996, 28–35.
6   Landen, S., 'Ariel document delivery: a cost effective alternative to fax', *Interlending and document supply*, **25**, 1997, 113–17.
7   Van Borm, J., 'From interlibrary lending statistics to clearinghouse: the use of ILL statistics in Belgium', *Scientometrics*, **25**, 1992, 89–100.
8   <http://www.libis.kuleuven.ac.be/libis/vowb/>
9   Van Borm, J., 'Performance measurement in document delivery: the case of IMPALA, the Belgian electronic document ordering system', *Proceedings of the second Northumbrian conference on performance measurement*, forthcoming, 1998.
10 Miller, W., 'Troubling myths about on-line information', *The chronicle of higher education*, 1 August 1997, A44.
11 Hastings, K. and Tennant, R., 'How to build a digital librarian', *D-lib magazine*, November 1996.
    <http://mirrored.ukoln.ac.uk/lis-journals/dlib/dlib/dlib/november96/ucb/11hastings.html>
12 Edwards, C., and Day, J.M., and Walton, G., 'Key areas in the management of change in higher education libraries in the 1990s: relevance of the IMPEL project', *British journal of academic librarianship*, **8** (3), 1993, 139–77.
13 <http://www.unn.ac.uk/~liy8/impel2/impel2.htm>
14 Edwards, C., and Day, J.M., and Walton, G., 'IMPEL project: the impact on people of electronic libraries', *Proceedings of the second electronic library and visual information research conference ELVIRA 2*, London, Aslib, 1995, 18–29.
15 Van der Auwera, F. and Van Borm, J. 'Training UIA library staff in the use of computer databases', *Health libraries review*, **12**, 1995, 65–7.

9

THE PROVISION OF LIBRARY SERVICES FOR LIFELONG LEARNERS IN UK ACADEMIC LIBRARIES

Jenny Craven and Shelagh Fisher

Introduction

The Study[1] on which this chapter is based was undertaken for the UK's Joint Information Systems Committee (JISC) of the Higher Education Funding Council, as part of the Electronic Libraries Programme (eLib). The aim of the Study was to define, compare and contrast a series of 'models' of lifelong learning and to examine ways in which UK academic library services could be developed to take account of the different models. The first section of this paper examines the concept of 'lifelong learning' and provides a profile of lifelong learners and the ways in which they are learning. The second part of the paper provides an overview of library provision for lifelong learners in UK higher education institutions and concludes with recommendations for the ways in which academic libraries might develop to support the lifelong learning process.

What is lifelong learning?

Lifelong learning and the learning society are not new issues. Some of the first ideas about lifelong learning can be traced back as far as the 1600s when Comenius wrote that 'no age is too late to begin learning'.[2] Other references to lifelong learning have been traced back to the 1940s[3] and more recently in literature dating to the 1960s and 1970s.[4] However, what was at one time a minority interest has exploded into world-wide significance: lifelong learning has become an important focus for society owing to factors such as the information society, the rapid expansion of new technologies, the rate of economic, industrial, commercial and even cultural change and, in the West, increased competition from emerging economies in South and Central America and Asia, where labour is cheap, plentiful and increasingly skilled.

The World Initiative on Lifelong Learning[5] was formed to develop the sharing of good practice relating to lifelong learning and to set and monitor standards for global lifelong learning. Many of the Initiative's activities were based on recommendations which emerged from the First Global Conference on Lifelong Learning in 1994. Initiatives include Community Action for Lifelong Learning (CALL), which outlines recommendations for sectors of the community and the Action Agenda for Lifelong Learning for the 21st Century[6] which includes the following recommendations:

- creation of learning organizations
- development of skills profiles
- initiation of individual lifetime learning plans
- provision of learning opportunities in lifelong learning
- creation of a learning passport
- improvements in accessibility to learning
- increased use of educational technology
- accreditation of courses wherever they take place
- initiation of portability in qualifications
- prioritization of essential new research.

As a result, there is a growing awareness of the need for individuals to take responsibility for their learning throughout their lives, and constantly to review and update their knowledge and skills. The current unstable job market means that people are often forced to reconsider their careers and learn new skills in order to keep up with employers' ever changing needs for skills.

The Campaign for Learning was launched in April 1996 by the RSA with an aim to create a 'learning society' by the year 2000. This learning society would see every individual in the UK participating in some form of learning throughout their lives and motivate people to take charge of their own learning.

More recently, lifelong learning has been placed firmly at centre-stage for higher education in the UK by the publication of the Dearing Committee's Report,[7] which has appeared under the title *Higher education in the learning society*. The first chapter is entitled 'A vision for 20 years: the learning society' and begins:

> The purpose of education is life-enhancing: it contributes to the whole quality of life. This recognition of the purpose of higher education in the development of our people, our society, and our economy is central to our vision. In the next century, the economically successful nations will be those which become learning societies: where all are committed, through effective education and training, to lifelong learning. [para. 1.1, p. 7]

A culture of lifelong learning will have implications for the delivery of all education and training, which must extend 'beyond the traditional institutions to include the home, the community, companies and other organisations'.[8]

The Department for Education and Employment and other government bodies are thus facing the challenge of lifelong learning. At the launch of Adult Learner's Week on 19 May 1997, the Secretary of State for Education and Employment, David Blunkett, stated that 'learning throughout life is becoming ever more essential as we approach the millennium'.[9] Since then the Government has announced its commitment to placing Further and Higher Education within a framework for lifelong learning through the proposed funding for one million Individual Learning Accounts for the support of learners. This initiative together with the development of 'Learn as You Earn' accounts is aimed to encourage private and public sector partnerships to help finance such schemes and to enhance learning and training opportunities for all. Individuals could also make contributions to their Learning Account during periods of time spent in employment prior to entry into higher education.

'Lifelong learning' is difficult to define. The term has been used in a variety of contexts, from 'adult learning' and 'continuing professional development' to organizational and societal change. Dictionary definitions of 'learning' per se are of necessity brief, but provide a starting point. For Chambers', to learn is 'to gain knowledge, skill or ability'[10] while for the OED it is 'a process which leads to the modification of behaviour or the acquisition of new abilities or responses, and which is additional to natural development by growth or maturation'.[11] Websters' definition is 'to gain knowledge or understanding of, or skill in, by study, instruction, or experience'.[12] 'Knowledge', 'understanding', 'skills' and 'abilities' are the outcomes: learning itself is the process.

Although education needs to operate within some kind of organized structure, it has been noted that 'learning is messy'.[13] People in general do not follow a set pattern once they have left the classroom or the lecture theatre: 'sometimes learning is simple, linear, conscious and brief, sometimes it is deeply unconscious and extraordinarily complex'.[14] The concept of 'lifelong learning' is no exception to these rules. It must be expected that this 'messiness' will become more and more pronounced as lifelong learning becomes embedded in society. Educators may try to impose order, as may governments and institutions, but individuals will follow their own motivations as they respond to the pressures, challenges and opportunities of learning. Ideas such as the 'learning bank'[15] which provide credits to be used throughout life will further empower individuals to define their own learning patterns. Rather than impose one 'model' on society, it is more fruitful to accept that lifelong learning needs to be messy and almost chaotic, subject to rapid change and largely self-determined.

Lifelong learning does not necessarily come within the framework of formal education. It takes into account all aspects of learning and provides a framework within which an individual can reflect on the past, undertake informal or formal learning in the present, and prepare for the future in terms of lifetime learning experiences. Learners are made aware that they are learning by aiming towards specific goals. Achievement of these goals becomes the motivation for what can be called 'deliberate learning'.[16] The distinction between one-off or day-to-day learning and lifelong learning is that with the latter, learners should retain what is learnt, and move on through life acquiring new skills to back up existing ones, rather than simply learning for a one-off activity, such as an examination or qualification.

The major characteristics of lifelong learning have been defined by Cropley[17] as:

- lasting the whole life of an individual
- leading to the acquisition, renewal and upgrading of knowledge, skills and attitudes to meet the needs of a constantly changing society
- being dependent on the motivation of the individual to learn
- acknowledging the contribution of educational resources available, including formal and non-formal education.

The need to integrate several types of learning has implications for higher education institutions who must accept that they make up just one small, but important, part of the system. Thus, a working definition of lifelong learning in the context of Higher Education could be:

'Lifelong learning is a deliberate progression throughout the life of an individual, where the initial acquisition of knowledge and skills is reviewed and upgraded continuously, to meet challenges set by an ever changing society.'

Who are the learners?

As the context of this paper is concerned with higher education, the focus is on adult learners. A recent UK survey[18] showed that 23% of adults are currently learning and a further 17% have been learning in the last three years. 48% learn for reasons connected with work and 36% for personal development reasons. Two-thirds of those studying, and three-quarters of people of working age, are aiming for qualifications. Ninety-three percent of people believe that 'learning is something people do throughout their lives'. Participation in learning is still skewed by social status and educational experience. Fifty percent of adult learners are middle class, 33% are skilled working class, 25% unskilled working class and 23% are unemployed.

Another study of trends in the learning society undertaken by Tett[19] revealed that adult participants in HE tend to be under 35, from skilled, managerial or professional backgrounds and have positive memories of, or tangible achievements from, school. Non-participation rates are highest from older age groups, ethnic minorities, those from semi- and unskilled occupations, those living in rural areas and women with dependent children.

'Mature' students are a very disparate group comprising, for example, women who interrupted their education to rear children, people wishing to pursue a change of career (either voluntarily or through redundancy), retired (or Third Age) individuals, professionals wishing to advance their careers, the long-term unemployed and those affected by significant life-changes (e.g. bereavement, financial loss). The diverse nature of 'who' the learners are has seen a growing demand for a more flexible approach to learning, with services such as open and distance learning courses available to students.

Why do people learn?

Learning may be seen as a route to a goal. The individual 'can consider what sort of person he wants to become, and what goals he wants to achieve, before making a choice between various alternatives'.[20] But learning is not simply motivated by individuals. Motivation may come from organizational workplaces or from societal requirements. The concept of a learning organization has arisen from the growing need for organizations to be aware of new developments and to harness new skills.

Organizations may need to change the focus of their business in order to compete effectively, they may need to become more aware of specific market forces in order to gain a competitive advantage. By supporting the learning process, the organization can take positive steps towards 'developing its potential by developing its workers.'[21] A learning organization environment can be achieved by supporting learning for the individual, department, team, section and ultimately the whole organization.

From a societal viewpoint learning has an important role to play. Part of the answer to the question, 'Why do people learn?' comes from the structures which societies build to encourage and enable their members to be learners. Motivations for learning can therefore best be understood as a complex mix of individual, organizational and societal pressures, desires and inclinations.

What do lifelong learners learn?

The survey of adult learning[22] found that 48% of adults are learning for reasons connected with work and 36% for personal development reasons. This suggests motivations for those undertaking professional/vocational learning activities (e.g. law, teaching, engineering, medicine), those pursuing discipline-based studies (e.g. history, English literature, philosophy, chemistry), those pursuing hobbies or leisure interests and those engaged in developing life skills (e.g. literacy, numeracy, decision-making, interpersonal skills). Crucial to the effectiveness of all of these learning activities is, of course, the process of learning how to learn.

Adult learning activity may be knowledge-based or skills-based, or a mix of the two. There is considerable debate about what constitutes appropriate professional/vocational education. The debate centres around how educational institutions, and in particular universities, should prepare students for life and work. Should it be through a general (liberal) education, or through more specialized profession-related training? From the middle of this century, a number of countries have established alternative institutions with a specific mandate to serve vocational training needs which the universities were not meeting. The Grandes Ecoles in France and the German Technische Hochschulen were established to provide highly trained professionals and technicians. In Britain, polytechnics were established in the 1960s with similar aims. As new universities, since 1992, much of the vocational/professional emphasis has been retained. Most recently in the UK, the DfEE has developed the Discipline Networks initiative, aimed at developing workplace skills for graduates.

Knapper and Cropley[23] suggest that lifelong learning would be facilitated by changes in the orientation and organization of the existing content of courses and identify a number of areas thought to define the minimum content necessary in a system devoted to lifelong learning. These include knowledge of communication, science and technology, the fine arts, ethics and citizenship, time and space and how to care for one's own body. These themes, it was suggested, should run through all courses and programmes to the maximum extent possible.

Where does lifelong learning take place?

Learning may take place at or away from an educational institution. Although traditionally learning has been institutionalized (nursery, school, college, university) it is now recognized that much learning takes place outside formal establishments and that such learning can be more effective, especially where it relates directly to the problem or work situation.

Although there are a variety of settings in which adults can learn , Tough[24] found that most adults felt that education and learning were not truly valid unless certified by a professional educator. Universities (21%) and colleges (20%) are the most cited locations for learning, followed by the workplace (15%), informally at home (10%) and adult education centres (9%).

The image of the 'traditional' route for higher education students has been full-time attendance, between the ages of 18 and 21, physically based within a higher education institution, usually away from the parental home, for a duration of three or four years, with minimal but adequate financial support. This model is being increasingly challenged 'by the accelerating changes in the once almost exclusive constituency of qualified school leavers'.[25] Changes have not only been in social and educational backgrounds, but also in modes of attendance. Students may attend courses on a full-time or part-time basis; be sandwich course , franchised course or distance learning students. They are benefiting from a range of initiatives and programmes which facilitate the lifelong learning process, including access courses, accreditation of prior learning, credit accumulation and transfer, accredited in-house courses whilst in employment, or partnership programmes between employers and higher education.

The problems which non-traditional students (such as part-time and distance learners) have to overcome are well documented in the literature. Problems faced by lifelong learners who are not students (either traditional or non-traditional) enrolled on formal courses of study are less well defined and indeed less well researched. The following section overviews current library provision in higher education institutions for both categories of lifelong learner.

Library services to lifelong learners

Elements of good practice in providing library services to lifelong learners who are registered as students (i.e 'non-traditional' students undertaking distance learning courses, franchised courses, or who are part-time) include reciprocal agreements between institutions, 24 hour opening, services provided by e-mail, fax and telephone, postal loans for books and journal articles, the availability of published guides informing users of facilities available, remote access to electronic information, and the provision of special collections of material for loan to such categories of user who are unable to visit the library to borrow material on a frequent basis.

Universities may have an agreement with other libraries which allow reciprocal use for reference purposes, or for borrowing. The Consortium of Academic Libraries in Manchester (CALIM) and the M25 Group in London are examples of university consortia which allow use by members of any of the reciprocating universities within the region. The SCONUL Vacation Access Scheme allows students from HE institutions throughout the UK and Ireland to use other libraries which belong to SCONUL (Standing Conference of National and University Libraries) during vacation times. The scheme provides access to books and journals for reference only. Restrictions on use of and access to electronic information are also common mainly due to the fact that 'licence agreements cover only members of the University'.

Courses offered on a distance learning basis frequently omit to provide information on access to the library's facilities. Information for study purposes is often provided direct to the distance learning students by the course tutors, in a repackaged form. The majority of institutions that run distance learning courses provide printed study materials as standard to course provision. In many cases, the printed materials are also complemented by electronic materials such as video, audio and computer software packages. Some institutions give the impression that students do not need to have access to any other supporting materials or indeed libraries, other than those supplied by the course. A statement indicating that 'course material is designed to be studied on its own without the use of library facilities' is fairly typical.

Distance learning students are sometimes encouraged to take responsibility for finding their own materials. At Kingston University, distance learning students of management are told that use of their 'own knowledge of a working environment can be useful as well as access to local libraries and companies and at Anglia Polytechnic University, distance learning students on radiography courses are 'advised to join public and hospital libraries as they will need access to a variety of reading matter'.

Information and communications technologies facilitate access to services out of hours. Heriot-Watt University for example offers LIBHELP which promises a response within one working day. Thames Valley University promotes its 24 hours a day learning facility with access to the library helpdesk via 'telephone, fax and computer'.

Libraries may also post items requested by mail to distance learning students. This facility is useful for distance learning students who may find it difficult to visit the library in person and libraries such as the University of Wales, Aberystwyth offer such a service. Other libraries allow students to renew items by post and by telephone. In some cases, although support for distance learning students is advertised, the library is still 'unable to offer a postal service for books or compensate totally for . . . not being able to access the services and collections in person' or will 'depend on . . . ability to visit the library in person'.

Sheffield Hallam University offers students a Distance Learning Support Service with a range of services to off-campus students, mainly from Management and Business related areas. The service offers distance learning support to students studying on courses that have been deemed as appropriate to distance learning. As well as sending out books and articles in the post to students, the service also offers book loans for up to three weeks, an inter library loan service and photocopying and supply of journal articles. Expansion of the service may see a move towards a 'network' of support with access to Internet based databases and OPACs, development of a database of academic library access policies and the possibility of offering services such as video conferencing. Special services for students studying at a distance may include short loan collections, which are 'purchased by the library specifically for distance learners'.

Students who are studying on franchised courses run by the University of Central Lancashire are able to use the services of the Virtual Academic Library of the North West (VALNOW) service which was launched in 1997. Based on the European Commission funded BIBDEL Project, VALNOW is the first attempt to replicate for students at a distance the library and information services enjoyed by their on-site counterparts. Students at participating institutions have access to electronic journals, browse the University's library catalogue and have loan items delivered by post to their local library. Requests can be made for photocopied periodical articles, and to access a range of online databases as well as the Internet. They are also able to draw on the subject expertise of specialist staff in response to reference enquiries, with electronic video-conference links bringing experts and students into a 'virtual' consultation.

Lifelong learners who are *not* members of a university may be granted access to the library provided they can demonstrate a need. The Robert Gordon University offers access to library facilities to potential external members who are 'studying for a professional qualification' or having 'problems in keeping up to date within your profession'. The University of Sussex allows 'various levels of service to non-members of the University, who can demonstrate a need to use a major academic library but have no access to one' and charges a fee 'for the provision of services on a cost recovery basis' rather than a flat subscription rate.

Restrictions on access in many cases depend on what subscriptions have been paid and which category the user belongs to, for example ex-staff may have different access rights from members of the general public or a separate fee may be charged for consultation and for borrowing. In some cases university libraries may restrict the number of external users allowing, for example, 'up to 30 members of the general public to borrow books from the university library'.

Some libraries will allow external users access to electronic databases, but access may be restricted and a charge may be attached. The University of Brighton for example states that 'access by external members is restricted to those databases not limited by type of user and to times when demand is low'. They also offer online searching at a charge upwards of £25.

Academic library services available to non-traditional university students are rarely planned with the attention given to the traditional, on-campus clientele. For such students, access to library resources is a very hit and miss affair. A few academic libraries have made great efforts and can demonstrate good practice but most treat non-traditional, or lifelong learners either as part of a general category of 'external readers' – or simply ignore them. This is very dangerous practice. If it is in fact possible to deliver distance learning effectively and efficiently without recourse to a library, why will we need libraries at all? Of course libraries will retain residual functions, such as places for on-campus study and archival collections, but they will be on the periphery of learning. It follows that there is a need for a concerted attempt to develop a basic set of services for the lifelong learner.

Developing academic libraries to support lifelong learning

Academic libraries, and university libraries in particular, have been at the leading edge of developments in the library and information world in the UK, especially in the use of technology to enhance information access and delivery. Initiatives at national and international levels to foster lifelong learning throughout society, regardless of age, social class and proven academic achievement are presenting new challenges which academic libraries can ill-afford to ignore. In order to meet these challenges, further developments are necessary to facilitate the provision of library and information services to the non-traditional, or 'lifelong' student. Potential developments for services, of information resources, of support for users and of library and information managers are discussed below.

Developing services

The trend towards convergence of the library and computing services within higher education institutions is now well-established. It now seems inevitable that academic libraries and computing services will need to provide a single interface to their users, so that guidance, help and advice can be provided regardless of the format of the information which is sought. The rapid development of electronic information sources has changed the nature of academic library provision in a very few years. Electronic sources can replace many of the traditional materials which libraries have used, especially in the area of datasets, some journals (an area where the trend to electronic formats will almost certainly accelerate) and new media such as webpages. However, there is almost universal acceptance that traditional formats (print, audio, video, etc.) will continue to play an important role in the total service which users require. From this has emerged the concept of the 'hybrid library', which may be seen as a new service model which provides *integrated* access to the full range of services. In the UK, JISC is funding a number of demonstrator projects in this area, starting at the beginning of 1998. For lifelong learners, as for others, this concept will have great importance in providing access to the widest range of resources in a manner tailored to the users' own requirements.

Lifelong learners are likely to access the campus less often than the traditional student or researcher. From that viewpoint, the library service they require will best be provided by alliances which enable them to use their own local libraries as their point of access. Especially in non-metropolitan areas which have a wide geographical spread, such reasoning will also lead to alliances between the academic and public library sectors.

Developing information resources

It will be necessary for academic libraries to shift their focus from form to content. Once users gain widespread access to information delivery services, they will wish to have access to content regardless of form, although they will also wish to be able to state a preference – which increasingly may be for electronic formats which can be manipulated within other documents. The library role will therefore be to facilitate content access as the primary concern. Managing this scenario will be a complex task.

The widespread availability of access to Internet resources, including the World Wide Web, has raised considerable concern about the quality of information which is being accessed. While printed publications go through a well known and tried and tested quality assurance procedure, involving referees, editorial boards and publishers' expert opinions, there is a lack of such procedure for electronic resources. In a situation where anyone can publish anything on the Web, it is difficult for users to judge the validity of the information they retrieve. The eLib Access to Networked Resources (ANR) projects are a partial answer to this problem, although at present their long-term future is not assured. Undoubtedly there is a role for systems which provide some kind of authoritative grading for networked resources, but at present it is unclear as to what that mechanism will be. Again, for lifelong learners, the need is likely to be acute as they may well be remote from sources of advice.

Information and communications technologies have much to offer the lifelong learner and may provide the boost which will make lifelong learning a reality. Libraries need to redouble their efforts to assist in the development of networked information resources and in their exploitation. However, the networked information arena poses questions about how users will be able to identify and retrieve particular information from the vast resources potentially available – the need is to provide the equivalent of a library catalogue which can be used as an access point to world-wide sources.

Developing support for users

The development of information handling skills is now recognized as central to learning. Included within these skills are the ability to identify information requirements, to develop and conduct a search, to retrieve information, to understand it and manipulate it, and to present information in a variety of contexts. Ways need to be found to ensure that all lifelong learners have the opportunity to acquire information skills, and develop their existing skills, so as to equip them to learn in the future.

Librarians have long struggled to try to make the service provided as relevant as possible to the users' requirements. For undergraduate courses this has often been epitomized by the annual struggle to acquire reading lists in time for books to be ordered and put on the shelves. With distance learning and franchised courses on the increase, librarians need to become more involved with course planning. They are able to bring new sources of information, and perhaps new learning tools, to the attention of teachers and to suggest ways in which the use of library services can contribute to the achievement of learning outcomes.

The essence of lifelong learning is that each individual will be undertaking learning of some kind throughout life. This provides an opportunity for universities to transform the relationships they develop with their students. Instead of the classic route of a three or four year undergraduate degree course, followed at best by a remote relationship through an alumni society, institutions will have the opportunity to persuade students to return again and again. It is a truism of marketing that it is far easier to sell another product to an existing customer than to recruit a new customer, and universities will need to grasp the opportunities this presents by developing lifelong relationships. The academic library could have an important role to play in these relationships, perhaps by transforming current 'external reader' membership arrangements into a new type of university membership which includes access to courses as well as to university facilities. Bearing in mind the large numbers of adult learners and scholars who are currently outside institutions, it may be that universities could use access to library services as a means of bringing such people into their communities in a much more active fashion than occurs at present.

Developing library and information managers

Overlaying all of the changes in academic libraries that a commitment to the support of lifelong learning will bring is that there will be a need for a high level of management skills. The administrative systems used by libraries need to be reconsidered as to their suitability for a service which is based as much on access to electronic information as on access to physical objects, and in particular where users are much more mobile and present their demands at a variety of service points across a network. Services must be expected to evolve rapidly, new technologies will need to be exploited, resources will be tighter than ever.

Conclusions

There can be no doubt that government and society are serious in their desire and intention to see the development of lifelong learning. Universities may embrace this concept enthusiastically or unwillingly, but they will not be able to ignore it. However, the changes that are required are so fundamental that at this early stage it is difficult to be certain of the shape of the higher education sector in the UK, still less of individual institutions. Libraries are, of course, parts of their institutions, not autonomous entities and it follows that their future is bound up with that of their parent bodies. There is, however, a further gloss to this apparently obvious statement, which is that each institution's library services will increasingly be seen simply as one part of the regional, national and international resource. Librarians have become familiar with the idea that many of their users will in future access these broader services directly, without using their local service as an intermediary or provider. Since many lifelong learners will spend less time on campus than the traditional full-time student or researcher, it is to be expected that they will make even more use of such unmediated services. The future of any one academic library service, therefore, cannot be regarded as merely dependent on the parent institution.

Having said this, the clientele which the library serves is likely to remain principally that of the parent institution. A question immediately occurs, therefore, as to the likely nature of these clienteles. It may be that some universities will see their future almost entirely as postgraduate and research institutions, while others will concentrate on undergraduate provision. One possible interpretation of this is that there will be a continuum of institutions, from those that are concerned almost entirely with postgraduate work and research, to those with very strong ties into the further education sector and an emphasis on access and wide participation. However it is more likely that we will see a series of innovations which will move institutions towards an ongoing relationship with their students, so that learning becomes a matter of students accessing courses at frequent intervals throughout their lives. Such a change could, of course, alter the nature of the institutions. In this chapter, we have tried to bring together some of the key issues for academic libraries which arise from the development of lifelong learning. In doing so, we have been aware of the need to tread a fine line between the need for 'bread and butter' traditional services to be made available, and the exciting prospects for transforming the role of libraries and librarians in the networked environment.

References

1 Brophy P., Craven J. and Fisher S., *The development of UK academic library services in the context of lifelong learning*, Draft report of a Study to JISC in the Electronic Libraries (eLib) programme, CERLIM/JISC, 1997.

2 Comenius, J. Pampaedia, in Longworth, N. and Davies, W. K., *Lifelong learning: new vision new implications new roles for people organisations nations and communities in the 21st century*, London, Kogan Page, 1996.

3 Giere U., 'Lifelong learners in the literature: adventurers, artists, dreamers, old wise men, technologists, unemployed, little witches and yuppies', *International review of education*, **40** (3–5), 1994, 383–93.

4 Cresson, E., *European Year of Lifelong Learning: presentation*, 1996. <http://www.ispo.cec.be/cgi-bin/vdkw_cgi/xafala5c0-1688>, 1996.

5 World Initiative on Lifelong Learning, *Lifelong learning: developing human potential: an action agenda for the 21st century*, Brussels, WILL, 1995.

6 Longworth, Norman and Davies, Keith W., *Lifelong learning: new vision new implications new roles for people organisations nations and communities in the 21st century*, London, Kogan Page, 1996.

7 The National Committee of Inquiry into Higher Education, *Higher education in the learning society: report of the National Committee* (Chairman: Sir Ron Dearing) London, HMSO (NCIHE/97/850), 1997.

8 Information Society Forum. Working group 4, *Education, training and learning in the information society*, 1996. <http://www.ispo.cec.be/cgi-bin/vdkw_cgi/xafala5c0-1719/>, 1996.

9 Blunkett, D., 'One million people will get £150 each for returning to class', *The Guardian* (Education supplement), 20 May 1997.

10 *Chambers' 21st century dictionary*, 7th edn, Edinburgh, W & R Chambers, 1990.

11 *The Oxford English dictionary* on compact disc, 2nd edn, Oxford, Oxford University Press, 1994.

12 Gove, Philip Babcock, et al., eds., *Websters' third new international dictionary of the English language* unabridged, Massachusetts, G & C Merriam Company, 1976.

13 Greany, Toby, 'Reaching our potential in a learning society: the Campaign for Learning assesses how we can learn to learn', *RSA journal*, **CXLV** (5479),

May 1997, 8–9.

14 Gear, Jane, [reported in] *RSA journal,* **CXLV** (5479), May 1997, 8.

15 Richards, Huw, 'Lucky election winners face cash hangover' *Times higher educational supplement,* 21 March 1997.

16 Tough, A., *The adult's learning projects : a fresh approach to theory and practice in adult learning,* Toronto, Ontario Institute for Studies in Education, 1971.

17 Cropley, A. J. 'Lifelong learning and systems of education: an overview', in Cropley, A. J., ed., *Towards a system of lifelong education,* Oxford, Pergamon, 1980.

18 Sargant, Naomi et al., *The learning divide: a study of participation in adult learning in the United Kingdom,* NIACE/ DfEE, 1997.

19 Tett, L., 'Education and the marketplace', in Raggatt, P., Edwards, R. and Small, N., eds., *The learning society: challenges and trends,* London, Routledge, 1996, 150–61.

20 Tough, A., *The adult's learning projects : a fresh approach to theory and practice in adult learning,* Toronto, Ontario Institute for Studies in Education, 1971, 45.

21 Raggatt, Peter, et al., 'From adult education to a learning society', in Raggatt, Peter et al., eds., *The learning society,* London, Routledge, 1996.

22 Sargant, Naomi, et al., *The learning divide: a study of participation in adult learning in the United Kingdom,* NIACE/ DfEE, 1997.

23 Knapper, C. K. and Cropley, A. J., *Lifelong learning and higher education,* London, Routledge, 1985.

24 Tough, A., *The adult's learning projects: a fresh approach to theory and practice in adult learning,* 2nd edn, Toronto, Ontario Institute for Studies in Education, 1979.

25 Silver, H. and Silver, P., *Students: changing roles, changing lives,* SRHE/Open University Press, 1997.

10

FOOLS RUSH IN: KEY HUMAN FACTORS IN OPERATIONALIZING SERVICE DELIVERY TO REMOTE USERS

Peter M. Wynne

Introduction

The development of library services to distant users at the University of Central Lancashire in the UK, began with the demonstration experiment conducted in the EC-funded BIBDEL Project[1] and led to the establishment of the Virtual Academic Library of the North-West (VALNOW), an operational library service to support the needs of students who are enrolled on University of Central Lancashire courses,[2] but who are based at a number of colleges spread right across the north west of England. The focus of this chapter is on conditions that apply in the UK further education and higher education sectors, but there is every reason to believe that experiences in the UK have wider application. Drawing on these experiences, this chapter explores some of the professional and personal issues which practitioners may encounter in seeking to extend library services from a large academic institution to smaller further education colleges and concludes with recommendations on best practice.

The needs of distance users are an imperative which is gaining momentum all the time, and the users themselves need accuracy and speed in information service because they are often constrained by factors other than study. The needs of distance users are clearly important, but there is a danger that as well as being *important* they may be in danger of becoming *fashionable*; and if that happens librarians will find themselves compelled by university managements to set up remote service delivery in double-quick time, with little regard for the pitfalls into which an embryo service can all too easily tumble. A key aim of this paper is to highlight a few traps for the unwary, in order that they may be avoided.

The BIBDEL Project

BIBDEL (Libraries without walls: the delivery of library services to distant users) was an EC funded Libraries Programme Project which inaugurated the Libraries Without Walls programme of conferences, and which was originally set up to investigate the LIS management issues contingent on the extension of library services to distant users. The Project ran for 18 months from April 1994, and the partners in the Project consortium were the University of Central Lancashire, Dublin City University and the University of the Aegean. At the core of the Project were three demonstration experiments which were conducted by each of the three partners to a body of 'remote' students.

In the case of Dublin City University (DCU), the demonstration experiment entailed students enrolled in the Faculty of Distance Education. This Faculty delivered courses to students all over Ireland who were allowed to use the DCU library but not academic libraries closer to their place of residence. The Project team at DCU set up an experiment which invited participation by Distance Education students, who already had access to computers in their homes or places of work, compliant with a certain basic specification.[3] The volunteers were given modems which allowed them to communicate with the researcher at the library, by means of an e-mail server and communications software which was contributed free by a Dublin software house for the duration of the experiment. Students could interrogate the catalogue, order books and journal articles for delivery by post and leave reference enquiries.

The University of the Aegean (UAe) was dispersed across four islands and had teaching departments and a library on each. Each library only contained materials to support courses taught by the departments on its own island. Similarly, the catalogue at each site only contained records for the local stock, and no union file existed at the time of the Project. As the University expanded during the early 1990s, students undertaking higher degrees, requiring cross-disciplinary reading matter, found it difficult to locate the whole range of their requirements. In order to address this problem in the Project, the UAe project team built a WWW interface which allowed searching of all four catalogues from any web-capable workstation. Requests for loans of material from another island's collection were coordinated by the Library Supervisor in Mytilene.[4]

In the UK, the University of Central Lancashire (UCLancs) chose Newton Rigg College in Cumbria for its demonstration experiment. The college at Newton Rigg was a further education college with particular strengths in land-based disciplines, based approximately 100 kilometres from the main Preston campus of UCLancs. Significantly, it was one of UCLancs Associate Colleges. UCLancs has partnership links with many colleges in the North, but Associate College status is reserved for the closest types of cooperation. Associate Colleges deliver UCLancs courses locally, through their own teaching staff, and their fitness to do so is validated by the University.

The experimental service was delivered to students enrolled on a number of UCLancs validated HE courses, including first degrees and diplomas in Forestry and a number of other environment-related disciplines. Services offered included access to the OPAC, the ability to request loans and journal articles and to submit reference queries, (and to receive answers from Project staff) all by means of a messaging module enabled on the OPAC. Books and articles requested by users were delivered to the remote College by post or fax. The experimental service also offered electronic document delivery and access to networked CD-ROMs.

The information technology was deliberately kept simple in all the demonstration experiments. One of the declared aims of the Project was to implement solutions which would be cheap, easily replicable and which utilized off-the-shelf products rather than commissioning expensive bespoke software. UCLancs' technology consisted of a 486 PC in the college library, a simple modem, a dial-up telephone line and a piece of communications software called Remotely Possible. This enabled the remote user to control a dedicated PC on UCLancs academic network which offered access, as do all the networked PCs, to the library OPAC and other library services. The messaging module on the Dynix library management system was in place on the UCLancs system but had not previously been used. Making it available for the experiment was simply a matter of getting an engineer from the system supplier to enable and configure it: a process which added two days external consultancy to the costs of the demonstration experiment.

In collecting and evaluating feedback from users following the demonstration experiment, the UCLancs project team found that all types of user gained from the experimental service.[5] Lecturers felt that the service helped in lesson preparation, their own staff development, and that students were on a more 'level playing field' than before, through access to additional and complementary material for coursework and dissertations. Students said that the service 'saved their time' and enabled them to undertake research on topics which were less well supported in their local college library. Lastly, the library staff perceived an 'expanded normal service' which offered windows on wider facilities both at and through the University, with access to international databases and networks including CD-ROM products.

VALNOW : The Virtual Academic Library of the North-West

VALNOW is the operational equivalent of the experimental BIBDEL service. Before the close of the BIBDEL Project, consideration was given to retaining the University of Central Lancashire demonstration experiment as an operational service. This was largely due to energetic lobbying from the librarian at Newton Rigg

College who had seen at first hand the advantages that remote access to library service could bring to distant users. During the same period, the University of Central Lancashire was considering its position with regard to the large number of further education institutions with which it had links of various types. Of these, the institutions most closely connected to the University were eight FE colleges throughout the North West which delivered University of Central Lancashire HE courses (either degree or HND programmes) locally, and which were known as Associate Colleges. These colleges stretched from Newton Rigg in the north of the region, to Liverpool in the south and as far east as Burnley in Lancashire.

The University Partnership Office devised an IT programme, known as the 'Partner College Information Strategy', to make electronic links between partner colleges (including the Associate Colleges) and the University, and to facilitate the exchange of various types of information including academic records, the University course catalogue and library and information services to Associate College students on University of Central Lancashire-validated HE programmes. A combination of these factors at a fortunate time resulted in the foundation of the Virtual Academic Library of the North-West (VALNOW) on 14 October 1996, and it has been operational since then.

VALNOW services

VALNOW offers its client colleges the following services:

- catalogue access
- book loan
- periodical article supply
- reference enquiries
- external information resources.

Catalogue access

Users can search the University's library catalogue by author, title and subject. The catalogue interface is exactly the same as that seen by an on-site user, and records show, in the case of loanable items, how many copies of each title the library has, loan type (normal, short or restricted), and loan status (in use, in library etc.).

Book loan

Users who require a loanable item from a catalogue search notify their college librarian who then contacts VALNOW personnel (by e-mail, fax, phone or post) and the item is issued and posted to the college. The college library notifies the user when the item is ready for collection. Off-site students are liable for fines at exactly the same rates as on-campus students, even if their college does not charge fines at all on their own stock.

Periodical article supply

Similarly, users (via their college librarian) can request photocopies of journal articles from titles which they have identified in University Library holdings. The article is then copied by VALNOW staff and posted or faxed to the college. The college library notifies the user when the item is ready for collection. The students are charged by their college for the copies at the rate which applies to on-site University users, irrespective of the college's local photocopying charges. A record is kept by VALNOW of the number of sheets of photocopy supplied to each college, and the college is recharged at the end of the financial year at the University rate.

Reference enquiries

Off-site users can also use VALNOW to submit reference enquiries which cannot be answered by the resources in their college library. These enquiries are referred to the college library staff in the first instance, but if they find they cannot provide a full answer the queries are passed on to the VALNOW service. VALNOW personnel then liaise with the appropriate member of the University Library's subject staff, to attempt to obtain a full response. Query outcomes are relayed back to the college for distribution to users.

External information resources

One of the advantages of the VALNOW initiative is that HE students at participating colleges are now able to access the Bath Information and Data Services (BIDS) databases, which have previously only been available to on-site users. The Associate College students use the same BIDS interface as on-campus students, via the Information Strategy IT link. Other conventional functionalities are also retained, such as the downloading to disk of search results and local editing and printing. The IT link also gives students access to the University's Internet server for WWW, Telnet and other Internet functions.

VALNOW and information technology

Information technology in VALNOW has, as in the experimental service, been kept simple and relatively inexpensive. The University's academic network is being extended to the colleges via a 64K bps kilostream link and a router at each college. Authorized users can therefore access some (though not all) networked services in the same way as an on-site user, including the OPAC. The use of the OPAC module for messaging as in BIBDEL has been discontinued, as the interface was difficult for users to learn. Messaging is now effected by e-mail, where colleges have this facility. Despite the similarity in their services to users, it is important to remain aware of the clear differences between BIBDEL and VALNOW.

Differences between BIBDEL and VALNOW

It has become clear from the University of Central Lancashire experience that the ethos of a research project is very different from that of an operational service. In a research project, rules can be bent or broken and *ad hoc* decisions can be made in order to accommodate the crises which inevitably arise in a new 'service' which has no benefit of precedent. In an operational context, far-reaching service decisions cannot be made in this *ad hoc* way, particularly when there is more than one external institution in receipt of services on an equal basis.

The conversion of services (which may have started as a finite research project) into a continuing facility thus needs careful planning, and any such planning process should take account of the human factors which the service will certainly encounter in its early stages. These factors apply to attempts to extend library services to distant users irrespective of whether the intention is to offer a fully integrated suite of full text, electronic document delivery services to a network of institutions, or merely postal loans to one small college.

In the following section consideration is given of some of these human factors which have been found significant in the transition from experimentation in BIBDEL to service in VALNOW. These considerations are presented in the form of a series of recommendations to any library considering setting up a similar service and are based on first-hand experiences of developing the VALNOW services at the University of Central Lancashire.

Human factors

Approach the client college as an equal

There is a gap between the HE and FE sectors in the UK, and as universities are on the advantaged side, FE colleges will be more aware of it. It could be argued that in the past the University of Central Lancashire Partner College Information Strategy has appeared somewhat high-handed from the point of view of the client colleges. There is a danger of appearing as the mighty university deigning to give humble colleges access to higher-level services. This is a gulf originally born out of a difference of purpose, thereafter of government funding, thereafter of perceived status. The UK further education colleges have historically delivered a heavily vocational curriculum, while even the newest of new universities have some sort of established academic record. Furthermore, it has been the mission of the FE sector to lead 16 to 19 year olds to their first post-school qualification, while the universities have concentrated on degree or similar level awards. Finally, while FE colleges are typically quite small institutions, serving the needs of a mostly local catchment area, universities are usually much larger and their recruitment is usually less geographically conditioned. It can easily be seen from the foregoing how these differences of purpose, funding and status have arisen.

There is consequently a necessity to consider one's approach very carefully indeed, even when speaking to fellow practitioners in the college library. I vividly remember, during the very early stages of VALNOW, writing to all the college librarians to notify them of a forthcoming meeting, the final details of which remained to be confirmed. I concluded my letter with a reference to Peter Brophy, the Head of Library and Learning Resource Services at the University of Central Lancashire:

> Professor Brophy's Personal Assistant will be writing to you separately to advise of the date of the meeting.

One of the college librarians was later to disclose to me that this mention of, in the first instance, a Professor, and in the second, one so powerful as to have his own Personal Assistant (both phenomena being completely outside her personal experience) was sufficient to awaken her grave misgivings as to the nature of the relationship which would exist between her college and the University in VALNOW. When I first met the librarian concerned, a great deal of reassurance was necessary to take the service forward.

Gather information before you start

At a very early stage in the emerging relationship between host site and client it is essential to gather as much information as possible. In planning VALNOW, we arranged to visit all the college libraries and librarians and sent them a questionnaire in advance. This was not a prescriptive document, but we used it to inform discussions during our visits. It was as much a chance to allow the college librarians to tell us what they wanted as for us to ask them questions. We also found it useful actually to see where services were delivered and where one's colleagues in the profession worked.

Talk to the right person

It is a regrettable consequence of the differences between the college and university sectors discussed above that librarians in colleges have lower status than their university counterparts. I was not therefore surprised to find that in the Partner College Information Strategy document the contact name for library matters in some colleges, after initial discussions between the colleges and University management, was a Vice-Principal and not a member of library personnel at all. This difference in status is related to the apparent high-handedness discussed above, which can often colour relationships between the two sectors. Practitioners seeking to extend services to college libraries where initial discussions have already taken place at management level on both sides should therefore note that the college librarian may know nothing of what has been agreed, and that a useful first step to open a genuine dialogue it may be useful for the university library representative to offer them a summary of progress to date.

The reason for poor communication in colleges is that the sector as a whole now carries a heavily political agenda. In the early 1990s, UK FE colleges seceded from local education authority control and were made self-governing. There is now a quite deliberate attempt to control communication to lower levels of management because of the risk of leaks of commercially-sensitive information to competitor colleges.

Be aware of, and sensitive to, differences in library administration

It is highly likely that there will be differences of library management practice between a university and a remote site, not least because of the differences between their parent institutions of size, function and budget. However, it should be noted that there may well also be less obvious differences in practice among apparently similar colleges in the case where services are to be extended to a group of new sites.

A couple of examples will serve to illustrate this effect. In setting up VAL-NOW we asked many college librarians how they approached buying books on the reading lists of the university-validated HE courses which their institution had been franchised to teach. Several librarians answered openly that their practice was to buy all titles immediately wherever possible. However, we were surprised to find that one librarian admitted with perfect frankness that she deliberately bought nothing in the first instance. She took the view that to buy books for HE courses which her FE students would never use was to subsidize the HE students to the detriment of FE provision. Her preferred strategy was to apply to the teaching department which was to deliver the new HE course for a vote of extra money, over and above the central library bookfund. It became obvious to the VALNOW team that, though this strategy was perfectly defensible from a professional viewpoint, not all college librarians had explored it.

A similar variation in practice was encountered in the matter of fines. Until recently UK Further Education colleges traditionally didn't fine users for late returned items, but more are doing so nowadays not least because they have found it to be a very successful way of encouraging circulation of stock. That notwithstanding, we encountered a range of reactions when we made it a condition of the extended service that the colleges charge fines at our rates and asked for their reactions. One librarian said he would impose them 'reluctantly' while another (who had already introduced his own fines system) said 'no problem – it will give me a good excuse to put my rates up!'.

Approach college librarians as an asset

It should be remembered that librarians at prospective remote sites are not merely passive consumers of extended services. There is much they can teach the host site: they know their own students needs and library use patterns better than anyone (certainly far better than the college teaching staff) and can use this knowledge in valuable ways, such as to predict demand for new services.

We encountered one college at which the cohort of HE students was a very small group compared to the rest of the student body. They were all part-time, and had daytime jobs. In addition, their classes were one evening a week only. The librarian therefore knew precisely when they would be in the library, and what services they would need.

Tailor the services on offer to the college library's technological level

In the main, UK FE colleges are not as advanced in terms of computer networking as universities. Consequently, it is useless to plan state-of-the-art networked services if colleges cannot make use of them, and overfacing a remote site with technology that they cannot exploit is not likely to encourage take-up of new services. Some colleges are admittedly very advanced; Wirral Metropolitan College has its own Intranet, for example, with access at 1800 workstations across 150 locations, but in our experience this is atypical. We assumed that we would be able to conduct much of VALNOW by e-mail (requests for loans, etc., and replies to users), but we found that not all of the eight client colleges had an external network connection and, of those that did, some had only one e-mail account for the whole college. None of them, even the most advanced in networking, was ready to allow students (or even just the HE cohort) individual e-mail addresses. Consequently, we resorted to low technology methods in some cases to ensure service delivery. It is better for the public perception of a new facility to have some sort of service running than none, while waiting for the technology at the other end to catch up.

Get agreement among partners

Ensure the services to be offered, the conditions they are to be offered on and the eligible users are agreed by all parties. In order to ensure this in VALNOW we formed a steering group of University personnel and at least one library representative from each college. Almost the first task in VALNOW was to establish written terms of reference for this group; who would be in it, when it would meet, what its powers would be. This was agreed by all parties. It should perhaps be stressed that these provisions are not set in stone, and can be varied, but their existence does help to formalize and give context to the group's activities. Next, the group decided on a Service Level Agreement: a document which makes explicit what services VALNOW would deliver and what was expected of the colleges in return. This was a lengthy process, but has been found very useful subsequently. For example, when we started VALNOW, at the University we decided that there would be no document delivery services (book loans and photocopies) to years 0 and 1 of the HE programmes, although they could use the other services. Document delivery was to be available to year 2 and above HE students only. The rationale for this was that we didn't want the University LLRS to be overwhelmed with off-site demand. In drawing up the Service Level Agreement, the college library representatives picked this stipulation out, and with the benefit of their better informed position, pointed out a multitude of reasons why it wouldn't be enforceable. We accepted what they said, as well as their prediction that we wouldn't be overwhelmed with demand, and scrapped the original stipulation. We've managed demand quite easily.

Publicize the service

Successful promotion of any new library and information service is very difficult, but after a certain critical mass of usage, demand can become self-perpetuating. However, in publicizing a new service at a remote site, don't assume word will get through to your client students, even if you design printed publicity material and leave generous supplies with the librarians at the remote sites. Librarians will do what they can, but they cannot always guarantee (especially in larger colleges) that publicity will get into the hands of prospective users.

A more thorough-going approach is to find out who the HE Coordinator is in each college, and preferably the names of the teaching staff who deliver HE courses. The host personnel should seek to establish good relations with the HE Coordinator and the teaching staff early in the life of the new service. This should be done by any means possible, but the preferred route is to go and visit them at the remote site. If you can, organize a presentation to the HE lecturers. This can be very difficult to do, owing to the heavy and increasing workload of lecturers but, if it can be done, talk to as many of them as you can. Let them tell you what their concerns and expectations are before you try and sell the service. Also, consider meeting the students themselves. Explore the possibility of giving a presentation to the HE cohort as they start their courses during induction week and consider offering conducted tours of your main-site library, so they can see at first hand what services will be available to them remotely.

The final human factor is taken from the rich comic repertoire of British pantomime:

Look behind you . . .

In other words: the threats and challenges which have to be addressed in setting up a service to remote users may not be obvious. It is as well to remember that, though the provision of services to distant users requires practitioners to adopt the perspective of looking outwards from their own institutions, the needs of users at the host library still require to be addressed, and the users themselves may not choose to ignore your best intentions to extend services to others. Furthermore, on-campus users may take the view that efforts to assist distant users may act to their own disadvantage.

At the University of Central Lancashire VALNOW was publicized in the internal University newsletter. In a personal email to the VALNOW Coordinator, a part-time student (who was also a member of the University's administrative staff) complained that on-site library users, like her, would be disadvantaged if prescribed texts were not available in the main site library, because they had been sent to partner colleges. It is advisable, just in case an allegation of this type is made, to have an answer worked out in advance. In this particular case it was pointed out in response that:

- VALNOW would, in any case, not lend short loan items (a category which accounts for most of the texts on course reading lists)
- VALNOW holds extra funds for the purchase of extra copies of texts in high demand at external sites.

Conclusions

So what conclusions can be drawn from these experiences in transforming a research experiment into an everyday service?

In extending an operational service from a large academic library to one or more external sites practitioners will inevitably be dealing with people, no matter how technologically advanced the proposed service may be. These people may include college management, teaching staff, college librarians, and students. Human factors – in other words the ways in which, and the conditions under which, practitioners interact with these groups – will therefore be crucial to success or failure. The lessons learned from our experiences at the University of Central Lancashire can be summarized very briefly as:

- treat the remote sites as equals
- assume nothing
- look behind you

and even more important . . .

- consult! consult! consult!

In the past, I think its fair to say that universities have been keen enough, for financial reasons as well as others, to enrol students at partner colleges of one sort or another, yet they've been rather less prompt at making appropriate library provision for them. It is not easy to set up a service to support distant users but, at the University of Central Lancashire, it was decided that there is a moral, as well as a professional, imperative to do so. The moral imperative is that these users are our students, registered on our courses, and we are in fact swindling them if we do not make a conscientious effort to allow them the same services as their on-site colleagues. The professional imperative is, to me at least, just as strong: that is we also hope that, through access to a wider range of materials and services than they would otherwise get, the learning experience of off-site students will be proportionately enriched. That is why, when the going gets tough and the users seem neither to know nor care about the services we can offer, or we find ourselves dishing out the same texts time after time, we should remind ourselves of this quotation from Gustave Flaubert:

> Language is like a cracked kettle on which we beat out tunes for bears to dance to, while all the time we long to move the stars to pity.[6]

I do not think it is too great a leap of the imagination, or too grandiose a proposition to suggest that, for our purposes, 'language' in that sentence can be seen to stand for the inheritance of which, as librarians, we are the appointed keepers: the sum of human knowledge.

References

1   Irving, Ann and Butters, Geoff (eds.), *Proceedings of the first 'Libraries without walls' conference, Mytilene, Greece, 9-10 September 1995*, Preston, Centre for Research in Library and Information Management, 1996, 28–31. [Deliverable Report 5].
2   Wynne, Peter M., et al., 'Delivering the library to its users: from the BIBDEL Project to the Virtual Academic Library of the North-West', *Interlending and document supply*, **25** (4), December 1997
3   Brinkley, Monica and O'Farrell, Jack, 'The delivery of library services to distance education students: the BIBDEL Research Project at Dublin City University', *The electronic library*, **13** (6), December 1995, 539–46.
4   Anon., 'Libraries without walls: brief programme description', *Bulletin of the Greek Library Association*, 1995. [In Greek. Unpaginated].
5   Butters, Geoff, et al., *Access to campus library and information services by distant users: evaluations of three demonstration experiments*, Preston, Centre for Research in Library and Information Management, 1996, 94–6. [Deliverable Report 3].
6   Flaubert, Gustave, *Madame Bovary*, quoted in Barnes, Julian, *Flaubert's parrot*, London, Cape, 1984.

11

THE LIBRARY EXPERIENCES OF POSTGRADUATE DISTANCE LEARNING STUDENTS OR *ALICE'S OTHER STORY*

Kate Stephens

Introduction

It is now some time since the Follett Report presented an imagined electronic future for university library services in which Alice, a young undergraduate, pursues her studies from a computer terminal in her study bedroom.[1] The idea for the Alice story, which is presented in the form of a fictional diary alongside diaries of 'The Academic' and 'The Virtual Librarian' in an aside to the report, was generated during the work of the information sub-group to the Libraries Review Group.

Follett's Alice wakes up to the sound of a bleeping computer in her study bedroom and breakfasts in front of a display of her latest assignment returned with comments in the margins from her tutor. She uses a plastic card to swipe in credit details and pay for electronic delivery of a recommended journal article.

> A quick breakfast and then Alice asks the computer to display her draft 'paper', (an anachronism since papers seldom are written on paper in this university), which had been returned yesterday with suggestions and comments from her tutor highlighted electronically in the margins. He suggests two further references. Alice switches to the library catalogue. Fortunately one reference is available on the campus textbook server: she requests it for printing in the hall of residence. The other reference takes longer to locate: it is an electronic journal article and will cost £10 for immediate transmission. Second groan of the day – her credit card limit is going to be stretched, but its urgent. She calls up the abstract/front page option on screen, decides it will be worth reading, swipes the credit card and in a few seconds the article is on screen, transmitted over the networks from an electronic document delivery exchange in Colorado.
>
> And so her day unfolds . . .[2]

Meanwhile, on the academic staff, Professor Higgins plans her electronic day, with little need for face-to-face communication. The person really in charge seems to be the librarian. The old library is now a car park, and the librarian's new role includes editing teaching resources, and developing hypertext links to catalogues, abstracting and news services, sample sets of data, and past exam papers and dissertations. He controls the copyright budget and is responsible for commercial promotion of the material produced. He seeks funds for research and development. He runs a weekly seminar on information recovery and management which he insists that academic staff attend with their students. It is a compelling picture, which puts the librarian very much in charge of a business which is as much about knowledge creation and dissemination as it is about information organization and retrieval.

The Follett Report seemed to present a vision of a changing learning environment, with implications for the distance learning student.[3] Yet, while the Report seemed to augur much for a technology driven convergence of conventional and distance learning, it appeared to have little grounding in the realities of distance learning as currently experienced. Indeed the Report made no specific references to distance learning. Librarians and academics involved in current distance learning practice can judge for themselves how far towards the Follett vision they have already moved. It is with the account of Alice's experiences that this paper is primarily concerned.

What follows falls into two parts. First is a vision of another Alice. This other Alice is perhaps the mother of the first. She is following a postgraduate course for professional development purposes, part-time, and at a distance from the course providing institution. The account is fictional, but is drawn together from empirical research into the current library needs of postgraduate distance learning students, which is reported more fully in the second part of this chapter.[4] The research project was conducted at the University of Sheffield from 1994 to 1996, directed by Lorna Unwin and Neil Bolton, and funded by the British Library. As well as the diary study which is discussed here, the research involved interviews with course providers, and surveys of university and public libraries.

A distance learning student's day (in which Alice rediscovers what it means to be a student)

Her children now grown up, and off to university, Alice decided to further her professional development by pursuing a masters degree by distance learning.

Half way through the course Alice discovered the need for a library. The course provided self-study materials along with a good deal of supplementary reading, but still there were points to clarify, and one or two things she would like to follow up out of personal interest. Already ideas were beginning to form for the dissertation, for which some wider reading would be necessary.

She hadn't much of a notion of what was available at the host university library. There had been vague talk at the introductory residential of registering with the library, but time had not been allocated for this and, after waiting for her personal tutorial on the Sunday, she could see, as she crossed to the car park, that the building was already closed. Perhaps it wasn't open at weekends at all!

Public library

She had a vague idea that the public library should be fulfilling some kind of a need here, and although she used her local library regularly for her own leisure reading, and for such things as holiday guides and consulting *Which?* reports, as well as to encourage the children to read, she was sure that the stock would have little to offer for the specialist nature of the course. She went nevertheless to see what was available. She noted the words FREE PUBLIC LIBRARY carved in stone over the rather fine art nouveau doors.

The librarian on the enquiry desk was interested in her situation, having once enrolled for a distance learning course herself. They shared a couple of experiences about the stresses and strains of doing such a course, found a useful basic text on the shelf, ordered a couple more references from the County Library via the local computerized regional catalogue, and processed three interlibrary loan requests.

It was difficult choosing the titles to order with, so far, a limited knowledge of the field, and not being able to browse. She was pleasantly surprised at how cheap it was (only 50p an item) but held back before ordering another five titles for the next assignment. On the way home, thinking about how long the librarian had said it might take, she regretted this. She hoped that the librarian would do as she had promised, and try to hurry things up in view of her situation. But she didn't really know how much influence the librarian would have, and wondered whether everyone could expect such special treatment.

Local university library

At home, she decided to take a bit more initiative and give the local university a ring. She was passed around several people before finding someone to answer her enquiry. When she was finally able to explain her situation fully, she felt that the words 'distance learning' and 'another university' had not gone down well. The response was unsympathetic: 'We have enough on looking after our own students without catering for the semi-detached variety'. It felt like a major setback, as if she was being treated as a non-person. She decided not to give up and planned a visit to her old university, 25 miles away, but a lot nearer than the one running her present course.

'Alma mater' university library

It was nice to be in a familiar place. She crept around rather guiltily not absolutely sure if she had any right to be there. Last time she came here it had been rather a quiet place. She remembered straining her eyes on the microfiche, getting the slide in the wrong way round and struggling with the up/down left/right adjustments of the screen, and having to consult the card catalogue for references earlier than a certain date. Now, students were queuing to use computer terminals which she supposed accessed the online catalogue, which she hadn't a clue how to use. It would be hard to spend a long time learning and making mistakes, with that queue growing longer behind. She didn't know if you needed some kind of password to get in. There was a small crowd of students jostling for attention at the enquiries desk. It was like a bazaar. Not at all the quiet and seemingly underused place of her undergraduate days.

She decided this time to chicken out on the catalogue and go straight to the shelves. She could have done with some direction in finding the right class numbers, but didn't like to ask for help in case she was asked to justify her presence. Browsing the shelves turned out to be more useful than she had expected. She didn't find any of the titles on her list, but found a later reference by one of the same authors, and spent a useful hour scanning some other related titles. She also found the current journals section and got side-tracked reading a completely unrelated piece about something her daughter was studying. She considered photocopying the article, but was put off by the queues and decided to leave it for another day, whenever that might be. She had to go anyway, but made a mental note that the library closed for the day at lunch time on a Saturday. She went home excited by the experience and determined to give her next visit priority, perhaps even over reading the course materials.

It turned out to be another three months before she felt she could afford the time for a second visit. This time she had a few hours owing at work. She decided to leave early in the afternoon and make an evening of it, when perhaps the place would be less crowded. The traffic on the motorway was worse than usual and she arrived, later than she had expected, at about four o'clock. She was dismayed to see that the library closed at five! Surely last time she had noted this as a day for late evening opening. Reading the notice with some care, she now saw the words 'In term time' and the dates showing that this was still (for some!) the vacation.

Suppressing the feeling of frustration, she planned at least to make the best of the hour she had. But something had changed. The porter on the entrance desk, had been replaced with an entry barrier with a sign reading 'Insert Card Here'. A notice beside the barrier directed students to another building to register for the new swipe card system. Students were fumbling in bags for their cards, and carefully passing through, as if the barrier had only recently been installed. A library assistant was standing nearby instructing students new to the system. Her plans to make furtive use of the library were completely scotched. No option but to announce her presence and find out what the proper rules were for using the library.

The library assistant directed her to a door marked 'Private' adjacent to the barrier. She introduced herself more cautiously this time than she had when telephoning the other place. She said she was a graduate of this university and that she understood she could make use of it as a former student in order to pursue some research of her own. The response wasn't quite so warm as at the public library, but she felt that the librarian was basically sympathetic, and rather apologetic that the rules were a bit tighter than they had once been. She gestured through the glass partition towards the queues at various points in the library and explained that an external reader's ticket could be offered at a reduced rate due to her former student status, but this would only allow borrowing a small number of books, and for short periods. The short loan collection and interlibrary loans would be unavailable.

It seemed like a lot of money, but she decided that this year's holiday fund would have to stand it. She couldn't help thinking, though, having financed herself through the course, she was paying for library services twice over. Once the forms were filled in and the cheque written, the library was about to close. This time she took a wad of information leaflets, including a guide to opening times and one about CD-ROMs available for student use. The librarian told her that a good time to come for a bit of peace and quiet was after the exams had started and before the summer courses began. There would be a window of a couple of weeks there when the place would be less hectic. It would still be officially term time, so the late evening opening would still operate.

When she managed the next visit, it was more like the library she remembered. There were no queues and she found somewhere to leave her things while she went off to browse. At first she just sat, gathering some thoughts about the direction she would like to take in her dissertation. She liked the smell of the place, and the sense of being connected with something she couldn't at the moment identify.

First strategy this time would be a database search. She had no experience of using computerized databases, but the subject librarian was happy enough to spend half an hour starting her off. Having joined officially, she now felt it was legitimate to ask for help. It took her a further hour and a half to download and print something that looked like a respectable database search. What if she had missed something? She wasn't confident that she had defined her terms well enough. She sensed that she would still have to find other ways of trailing the key material.

A search of the library's own catalogue showed her the limitations of the library she had just paid to join. Hardly anything of relevance turned up in the OPAC. Her first reaction was to feel she had been cheated. Remembering her experience on the first visit, she went back to the shelves and found one or two relevant titles and a collection of papers by a relevant author which had not turned up in the search. From a quick flick through a periodical she had not heard of before, she found two papers that she could see were immediately relevant to her study. At least the journey was not wasted, but there was one key reference from the reading list, which was referred to in some of the material she had found, and which she knew she must read in order to see how present approaches to the field had come about. She knew now that the next stop would have to be her own university. They, surely, would have a collection more comprehensively covering her field of study. If they didn't keep this particular reference, she knew she would be able to ask them to get it through inter-library loan.

Host university library

From home, she made one or two telephone calls and finally spoke to the subject librarian at her own university. The librarian was prepared to admit that, yes, distance learning students have a problem, and, yes, as a special concession to her she would personally photocopy a couple of references and send them, along with a key monograph, by post, as long as she was able to pay the return postage. She was sympathetic to the problems, expressed some concern about students sticking too closely to a narrow range of material, and course providers not thinking things through. Surely, they both wondered, universities who had been around in distance learning longer would have sorted this one out?

The librarian also said that, with the expansion of courses like hers, the university was considering ways of improving services, but this would depend on additional staffing. Existing staff were pressed enough as it is. She looked forward to the day when distance learning students could search databases from home and make e-mail requests for material to be sent by post. She said that the university had an experimental project looking at just this, but of course not all students had access to the technology, and when they did there was always the problem of training and technical support.

Alice wondered whether these developments would increase the demand to come and look at books, rather than reduce it. She was beginning to think of her guilty and unannounced presence in her old university library more as the exercise of a basic freedom browse. She was thinking of her own success in extending the boundaries of a reading list and a computer search by defining relevance for herself. She was beginning to remember that this was one of the things you were supposed to learn at a university. She wondered, half seriously, if the day would arrive when an adult learner's version of a mass trespass would be needed to secure the rights of citizens to access a national resource of materials for lifelong learning in libraries.

The diary study

The account above is based on insights gained from a research project, including the findings of a diary study involving a group of postgraduate students over periods ranging from three to 12 months. The study provided dramatic evidence for the battle with time, institutions and resources, which many distance learning students face. It illustrated the sometimes clandestine nature of distance learning students' library use, while confirming the value which students place on making personal visits to libraries in order to browse books on shelves. In addition, the study suggested that the burden of arrangement for library provision is not currently being fully met by providing institutions, with other universities, public libraries and specialist libraries fulfilling most student needs.

The 47 postgraduate distance learning students involved in the study kept records of their library use between January and December 1995, for periods of at least three months. Of the sample, 35 continued for six months, 22 for nine months and nine completed diaries for a full year. The students' homes were widely spread across the UK. Ages ranged from 26 to 51, with an average of 39. The majority (30) were female. They were following courses, delivered by 12 dual-mode universities, in a range of subject areas, including Education, Management, Library and Information Science, Law and Medical related courses. Between them, the diarists returned 830 records of library use.

The number of years participants had spent in higher education prior to the current course varied from none to 10, with 3 being the most common response. Professional experience averaged 15 years, with a range from 4 to 30. Training in library use varied from having never received any at all, to very extensive for a participant holding a senior position in an academic library. In all, 6 participants relied totally on previous experience of libraries in earlier courses, having received no training as part of the current course. A further 13 had received no training other than an information pack about the library.

How libraries were contacted

For each record of library use, participants were asked to indicate the manner in which they had made contact with the library – whether by visiting in person, or through another person, telephoning, using the post, or making contact via a net-

Table 11.1 *Ways of contacting the library*

	Number of times library used	Percentage of diary entries
By visiting in person	585	70.5
By telephone	142	17.1
By post	72	8.7
Through another person	21	2.5
By online sessions	28	3.4
Total	848*	

*This figure is greater than the number of diary returns because in some cases the same return was given more than one code.

worked computer from home or work. They were also asked to indicate how much time had been spent in the process.

Table 11.1 indicates how many times each of the above ways of contacting the library were reported. The table shows that by far the most common way of making use of the library was by personal visits, which account for the vast majority of the diary records. The next most common mode of contact was by telephone, with postal and online contacts representing only a very small proportion of the records.

For 741 of the diary entries, a time was given for the period of use. Overall, the diarists recorded 666 hours and 25 minutes of library use. The average recorded length of use was approximately 54 minutes, with the longest record being seven hours. Out of 563 personal visits, a total of 614 hours and 10 minutes was recorded, with an average time for personal visits of approximately 65 minutes. Table 11.2 gives times in minutes for all the recorded modes of contact.

Overwhelmingly, these students are making use of libraries by visiting them in

Table 11.2 *Contact times*

	No. of records	Percentage	Total time, min.	Average, min.	Maximum, min.
Personal visits	563	73.6	36,850	65.45	420
Telephone	136	17.8	1,745	12.8	180
Post	23	3.0	195	8.48	60
Another person	18	2.4	320	17.7	120
Online	25	3.3	995	39.8	180

person. A number of themes arise from the comments they make regarding these visits. These themes are elaborated under the headings below.

Telephone contact

Use of the telephone was the second most frequently recorded means of contact. Its use was described for a variety of purposes, including enquiries about opening times, renewal of books on loan, requests for photocopies or books to be sent by post and requests for literature searches. Comments varied between the delighted and the frustrated:

> [The librarian] is always so obliging and is able to answer queries. She always tries to get what you order and never appears to get tired of requests. (She gets a lot from me.)

> The lady who answered was very abrupt and told me she hadn't time to answer the phone and take details as she was busy – so ring next term when the students were back or better still call in next term and use the library myself. I was very angry . . .

By post

Only 3% of diary entries recorded use of postal services. Those who did use such services sometimes described great pleasure in receiving much wanted books by post.

> At last. Just when I really needed it. I have until 20 July but I will be finished with it by then – great.

However, problems were noted connected with the receipt of books by post.

> Unfortunately, only one of the three books I received was really useful. Postal borrowing is an expensive way to browse.

Visits by other people

Reliance on other people to gain access to books was sometimes mentioned, reflecting a similar strategy highlighted for Australian distance learning students by Winter and Cameron.[5] For example:

> My daughter is a student at ——— so she said she would look for a book for me.

Unfortunately the library stock was very limited.

Online access

Access to library services via a networked computer from home or work, account-ed for a similarly small proportion of library contacts (3.3%). Of the comments relating to online contact, the majority concerned the use of electronic mail. This confirms the finding of Ladner and Tillman that even for specialist librarians, the most frequent use of networked computers is for electronic mail.[6]

E-mail to librarian re library search she is conducting on my behalf.

I now have e-mail on laptop at home so can communicate with librarian whenever the urge takes me.

Sent list of six books/articles to house librarian via e-mail.

The following comments, all from the same person, concern difficulties in gain-ing online access for other purposes:

Access gained to —— but couldn't get access to other libraries from there. Disappointing and time consuming and probably expensive. Will discuss with com-puter staff during summer school.

I originally thought that I would be able to access various journal databases and do searches of contemporary material. However, so far it appears that although I can get into various library catalogues for books, I cannot get any journal databases. This is a large disappointment because it appears I'm going to have to continue to wear out shoe leather and beg physical access to local universities and pretend to be a real student so I can use CD-ROM services.

This is where I get frustrated. I don't think I know enough about the technology to make full use of it and the longer I'm using the connection the more concerned I become about the cost.

Use of the various types of library

Diarists were asked to indicate the library to which their comments related. Table 11.3 shows the number and percent of comments relating to the various types of library used. Clearly, these diarists are making extensive use of libraries of universities other than those which deliver their courses. The second largest frequency concerns specialist libraries of various kinds. Frequently, these are libraries run by professional organizations or services.

Public libraries

While the diary group seemed to make proportionately less use of the public library service compared to the student questionnaire sample as a whole,[7] nevertheless the public library seems frequently to be regarded as a good place to study and a valuable source of material, as the following comments reveal:

> This is a very small branch library, but it's always worth checking just in case. I did get one book which is relevant.

> No suitable finance or banking books – but OK for social sciences . . . I'm surprised by the number of suitable books a small public library . . . holds . . . It's also a pleasant place to work and the staff are generally helpful.

One diarist expressed her frustration with borrowing restrictions:

> decided to see if the lending library was any good. Again same OPAC and some of the titles I need are available. Looks more hopeful. Also did author search and found one or two not on my lists but potentially interesting and useful. Good. Joined up and proceeded to locate five books – three of them on my list. Then came the crunch – because I live and work outside the city boundary (only one and a quarter miles away) I can only have three books at a time. If I worked or lived in the city I could borrow 12 at a time. How phenomenally frustrating! The staff were generally pleasant but when I asked to see the Chief Librarian or someone with whom I could

Table 11.3 Comments relating to types of libraries

		Percentage
Host university	122	14.8
Other university	290	35.2
Specialist library	200	24.3
Public library	137	16.6
Further education	73	8.9
Other	2	0.2
Total	823	

explain my needs . . . the shutters came down. Rules are rules, we can't make exceptions . . . why not try writing – all these and other equally frustrating remarks. Not the most relaxing way of spending several hours of a much needed three day half term, especially when I had hoped to get some serious reading done.

But apart from situations like this, several comments suggested a high regard for the public library service, and indicate the manner in which its use can be a family affair which is integrated with other aspects of life:

> This is probably off the point but is a word in favour of my wonderful local library. I had reserved a book for my daughter's school work which was found to be out of print and difficult to obtain. In two weeks it was located for me . . . and was waiting for me to collect. This service was provided free of charge and with courtesy and a smile. If a little library can go to that effort for a six year old, I think it is an excellent service . . . I may follow up the possibility of them finding texts for me, as I walk past this library every day on my way home.

Host university library

While the host university library seems to have been used a little less than public libraries, several entries were made regarding its use during residential periods or special visits:

> This was during the residential weekend. A request had been made for the library to be open for longer than the two hours on the Saturday afternoon as on previous occasions – so we got three hours. I didn't find it easy to find the documents I had tried to request the previous day – in fact only two of the five as other people were wanting them as well – had to queue for a ticket to use the photocopier and then the queue for the photocopier was long so gave up and went in search of other material. I never used my ticket so wasted my money.

One student pointed out that the study school may not be the best time to select material:

> During the study school I really felt no pressing need to use the library – excellent though it is. It is not until I actually start working through the modules that I need library services.

Having made a decision to commute to her host library at a critical stage in the study, this student experienced difficulties:

I did not realise it was the end of term, the library is packed with students desperately trying to complete assignments. I couldn't get near a PC to carry out my search. (I should have thought about the timing of the visit, I had spoken to people at the university but no mention was made of difficulties accessing services at this time of the term.)

Complaining of difficulties regarding loan periods for distance learning students:

I was told this system is geared to the full time students and could not be changed. (So much for equality.)

In the absence of any postal service, one diarist said this:

how can a DL student use a specialized library which is 108 miles away from her home (two hours drive each way) and only borrow books in person – yet have to complete assignments where one of the criteria for marking is for evidence of further research beyond the set books.

Libraries of other universities

Over one-third of the records returned concerned visits to university libraries other than the host library. There can be problems gaining legitimate access in the first place. One student relied on her friend to get her inside a library which has introduced restricted access. Another student described at length the problems she had in renewing a reader's ticket and the response she received to a request to extend borrowing rights:

I arrived today with the final book ready to discuss my case with the most senior person available if my card was still trapped. It was cleared as soon as the book went in. I asked about the date of expiry on my card and was told that it was up. The librarian offered to extend my card until August 1995, but once again warned me that the external readers cards were 'under review'. I heard this phrase on the first day I received the card, which I believe was in June 1993. I questioned her further today about why this was continually under review and was told that the library's first priority was to their under and postgraduate students. If too many demands were made from outside sources the students would suffer and the library would be failing to meet their needs. I asked for both an extension to the number of books I could borrow at one time and the time for which I could keep them. There was no leeway on either. The levels had been agreed by the sub librarians of each campus and were inflexible. I was also informed that many people were refused cards. Think yourself lucky . . . !

Sometimes access to short loan collections is completely denied to the external reader, as is access to computerized databases. While problems with insufficient loan periods for normal stock books were mentioned, some people clearly experience little difficulty in this area, relying on good relations with library staff:

> . . . I went in to make my apologies and renew the books. This can be done over the phone but I always prefer to go in person and speak to the librarian as I feel it maintains a good relationship. I chatted about my work (which is a few weeks behind schedule at the present) and was on my way. The librarian knows me well enough by now and was not at all cross with me.

Use of personal connections can be a strategy used in order to get access, but this diarist couldn't help being angry at poor communication, despite professional sympathies and feeling guilty about lack of entitlement to access:

> Returned very angry. [The library] was being completely revamped. When I arrived, I found the system was down and there was no access to bookstock. I asked at the counter and the assistant was very pleasant and said that there had been notices up for some time warning about this. Unfortunately as I don't go that frequently I had no way of knowing. So a long journey specifically to get items to use over the vacation was semi-wasted. Why couldn't I have been warned of this when I rang earlier in the week? Fortunately I could do some photocopying, but when my card ran out, they refused to give me change. I know this is a policy (we do the same) but it was quiet, just before Christmas – what about a little goodwill? Too annoyed to complain (also that feeling of not really being entitled to access) . . .

Specialist libraries

Almost a quarter of the records returned concerned use of specialist libraries, including professional and workplace libraries. Limited though such collections may be, students seem relieved to discover their potential, sometimes after frustrating experiences with university libraries:

> My organisation (a social work training agency) has a small in-house library. There are now few recent books but there is a reasonable collection of reports, journals and newspapers. We also have a daily press cuttings service. Through the librarian I have access to the British Library Lending Service which is my life line!

The same diarist commented:

I have never used work library [sic] before my course – now it is a place of refuge.

After several entries recording use of this library, she reported:

> Have just heard that as part of a cuts package required by government, the library
> is to be closed – probably at the end of March. From a selfish point of view I won-
> der how I am going to complete my degree. From a professional point of view I can-
> not believe that an organisation with a statutory responsibility for education and
> training should be expected to manage without a library. Couldn't establish what is
> really going to happen. Is the library closing? Is the librarian to be transferred? What
> will happen to the British Library subscription? . . . I wonder how many libraries
> have suffered a similar fate in recent years.

The value of browsing

A clear message from the diaries is that students value the opportunity to visit
libraries in order to browse the shelves and keep up to date with journals. The
importance of this activity in getting a feel for relevant material when specified
titles are not available, and for enlarging the reader's thinking outside given categories is emphasized in several of the comments.

> I returned all the books I borrowed and spent about an hour browsing through the
> school science book shelves. Normally I would use the LIBERTAS computer index
> to search for books. In this case I was happy to just skim through books and choose
> the most appropriate.

> Decided to have a quick scan along the shelves of my area of interest. Picked up two
> 1995 publications. It is exciting and stimulating to use a library which is purchasing
> books in one's area of study. I get great pleasure from my library visits. I only wish
> I could spend more time there. However, limited time has its advantages in making
> me think more methodically and more precisely what exactly I am looking for. With
> more time I would get distracted and 'waste time' on all the things I see and think
> – 'that looks interesting'.

> Check subject index and browse shelves and find a few interesting and useful back-
> ground documents. Great believer in browsing.

> Eureka! It's amazing what you can find on the shelves if you really look.

> Just pottered through library related subjects and browsed shelving and catalogues

getting rough ideas for dissertation topic.

Library use as a clandestine activity

A distinctive feature of distance learning students' library use is that they operate around the margins of normal institutional services and practices. Library use does not, for most such students, occupy its own rightful space, but instead runs in parallel with whatever other life demands permit, or is slotted into the spaces which are left after the demands of daily and work life are met, and institutions have fulfilled their functions regarding normal students.

This is evident from the questionnaire responses which indicate that some students do not consider themselves 'real students' and would like to be treated 'normally'.

From the diaries there is evidence that libraries are used in the nooks and crannies of space that are left between the demands of family and professional life.

At its best this jigsaw puzzle of demands results in an integrated picture of apparently harmonized reading opportunities. One diarist presented an account of visits to libraries in which professional demands, his children's development, his own personal reading and the demands of his course are all neatly dovetailed together. Another diarist seems to see herself as operating at the edges of legitimacy by taking her daughter to a university library:

> I had my twelve year old daughter with me who was going to do her homework while I carried out my own business. She felt uncomfortable as there were notices prohibiting school pupils from using the library as a study area. This was presumably due to lack of space but I was prepared to make a request for her to stay if we were challenged – we were not.

The experience of operating at the edges of what is acceptable is also evident in the following extract where borrowing books has the air of an act of theft, rather than a wholly legitimate affair:

> Now it is the school holidays. I had two little girls with me (the baby is in nursery full time so he is no problem) I sat them in a corner with some scrap paper, pens and scissors and told them to be as quiet as mice! In these circumstances, I have to find what looks promising as quickly as I can and then I can review it properly at home in my own time.

In the following comment the pressure of other commitments, and the sense of using the library furtively, as if under cover of darkness comes across!

> A very quick visit to the library en route to parents' evening – I would rather be in the library! Many of the visits to the library are quick ones in the evening after work. It would be a delight to spend time during the day just browsing.

In the following comment spending time in the library seems pleasurably indulgent:

> I found myself with an unexpected afternoon off and it is the last day of school term so I indulged myself in simply sitting and writing. I have always found the library a helpful place to write since being an undergraduate and spending days in libraries. Today I did it with a sense of indulgence and really enjoyed myself.

Librarians are as susceptible to the feeling of operating in a grey area as are other students:

> A rare use of the enquiry desk. As a librarian I feel I should be able to work most things out for myself. Also I still have a guilty feeling that I'm not really supposed to be using the library. A more formal arrangement would assuage this guilt.

The pressure of time

Confirming the findings of the larger scale questionnaire survey the diaries revealed that time can be the single most pressing concern for these students.[8] Almost 10% of the diary entries made some reference to time constraints and this emerged as the most frequently mentioned theme. Among these were repeated complaints about university library opening times:

> I was resident at the university 24–28 July in order to work on my dissertation. Horror! Only the Education Library was open – others . . . were all closed for stock-taking.

Others were more concerned about their own sense of having insufficient time:

> Three hours passed very quickly and I walked away with a fair heap of material. Unfortunately I felt rushed all the way through the visit and feel I could have benefited from a longer visit. However, with a full time job and only a few days in London long visits to libraries are rarely possible.

This comment reveals another aspect of time pressure:

> I could take another two and a half years to write the dissertation, but getting the degree this year improves the renegotiation of my contract of employment, which is why I embarked on the course. I will still take two years after that to become chartered – I'm already 42, how old do I want to be when I'm finally qualified.

Conclusions of the diary study

The returns suggest that there remains a heavy weighting towards using libraries by making personal visits to them, despite forecasts of the imminent demise of the library as a physical place.

The most frequently used library resource remain the libraries of other universities rather than the host. Problems of access include entrance barriers, restricted external borrower status, limited loan periods, difficulty associated with short loan collections, unfamiliarity with local systems, lack of information about systems and practices and absence of relevant stock. Better access is sometimes gained through personal connections. Concessions regarding the rules for use and borrowing can sometimes be gained through friendly contact with a sympathetic librarian.

Specialist, including professional and workplace libraries form the second most commonly used for this group. Despite sometimes limited collections, their use can be associated with a sense of relief after the battle for access to a university. The existence of such libraries is sometimes under threat from institutional reorganization.

For the group who participated in this study, public libraries were third in order of frequency of use. There is a commonly expressed view that the middle classes have abandoned public library borrowing in favour of buying books for personal collections. This study provides some evidence for the esteem and affection in which the public library service is held by the adult learner. It seems to remain an important source of academic material, and for some its use is integrated with family activities, such as children's reading and shopping. The role of the public library service needs better recognition and support.

The host university library was less frequently used that the other three groups. Problems in the use of the host university library include both distance and inconvenient opening times, when students visit either for organized residential courses, or by their own arrangement. Breakdowns in communication regarding when facilities will be available sometimes occur, with libraries typically geared to the demands of the timetable of full-time, on-site undergraduates.

Postal services are valued where they exist, although the cost and the waste involved in ordering material which turns out not to be useful or relevant can be seen as problems. Getting information and making arrangements by telephone varies in success. The pleasure and relief at saving unnecessary and wasted journeys through use of the phone is mirrored by the extreme frustration experienced when the telephone response is unhelpful.

Several mentions were made of the use of networked computers in order to obtain library services. Where this group used such facilities it was most frequently for electronic mail. One student described the disappointment she felt at being unable to access databases through an Internet connection with her host university library.

The need to browse books on shelves came across strongly from these diaries. In addition to a concern with time pressure, which mirrors the findings of our questionnaire survey, this study has revealed a clandestine aspect to library use for distance learning students. The diaries suggest that library use for these students has an air of illegitimacy. Students see themselves as operating outside the normal expectations of academic and student life, and hanker after a legitimization of their study needs. It may be that in part this sense of illegitimacy can be partly alleviated through better communication and training.

Students want the opportunity to browse for extended periods before deciding what to take home and read in depth. Access as external borrowers to nearby university libraries can be expensive and limited in the services which are offered. Use of networked CD-ROMs, for example, may be excluded. But even if these difficulties can be overcome, the stock of a local institution may not reflect the reading demands of a particular course. Despite this, extensive use is being made by this group of local university libraries, in excess of the use made of the host university library.

A vision grounded in real students' needs

In technological terms things are moving fast, but not so fast that the current needs of students can be ignored. In the national press, visions of technology driven convergence of conventional study with distance learning, in which technology renders the need for physical access to places of study and their resources unnecessary, is frequently repeated. For example, Revell quotes views of educationists which ally this vision with the opening up of educational opportunities.[9] But while visions proliferate, real experiences are being neglected.

Our studies suggest a model for provision which emphasizes integration of technological developments with traditional means of library access. Current patchy and inequitable access to networked computers for catalogue and database access and document delivery will only increase students' need and desire for access to real books on shelves. Real books will be needed not only for access to full text, but also for the serendipitous aspects and the more corporeal pleasures of reading.

While the North American library community seems to have opted for placing the responsibility for library access with the course providing institution,[10] in the UK we are uniquely placed for a balance of provision of services with three focuses: the public library, which our studies suggest is well used by the distance learner; nearby higher education institutions, to which adult learners have a traditional informal right of access for browsing; and the course providing institution. The first of these, should be funded for the purpose. The public library service has always had an informal role as a 'people's university', and since the beginnings of the Open University at least, there have been concerns about its lack of funding for this purpose. Rights of access to the second could be formalized by a National Library Card scheme, as envisaged in Australia,[11] which might counteract the currently increasing restriction of access imposed by the introduction of electronic barriers at entrances. The last could take a coordination and training role, in some cases relinquishing a portion of the fee which a student might need in order to gain services elsewhere. In balancing these three foci of provision, the librarian's role in both training of students and liaison with academic staff in course planning will be critical.

References

1   HEFCE, *Joint Funding Council Libraries Review Group Report*, HEFCE, 1993.

2   HEFCE, *Joint Funding Council Libraries Review Group Report*, HEFCE, 1993, 60.

3   Unwin, L., Bolton, N. and Stephens, K., 'The role of the library in distance learning: implications for policy and practice', *Library and information briefings*, **60**, 1995.

4   Bolton, N., Unwin, L., and Stephens, K., *The role of the library in distance learning: a study of postgraduate students, course providers and librarians in the UK*, British Library/Bowker Saur, 1998 forthcoming.

5   Winter, A. and Cameron, M., *External students and their libraries: an investigation into student needs for reference material, the sources they use and the effects of the external system in which they study*, Geelong, Deakin University, 1983.

6   Ladner S. J., and Tillman H. N., 'How specialist librarians really use the internet', *Canadian libraries journal*, **49** (3), 1992, 211–15.

7   Bolton, N., Unwin, L., and Stephens, K., *The role of the library in distance learning: a study of postgraduate students, course providers and librarians in the UK*, British Library/Bowker Saur, 1998 forthcoming.

8   Bolton, N., Unwin, L., and Stephens, K., *The role of the library in distance learning: a study of postgraduate students, course providers and librarians in the UK*, British Library/Bowker Saur, 1998 forthcoming.

9   Revell, P. 'The people's university', *Guardian higher*, 13 January 1998.

10 Stephens, K., 'The role of the library in distance learning: a review of UK, North American and Australian literature', *The new review of academic librarianship*, **2**, 1996, 205–34.

11 Crocker, C., 'Meeting the information needs of external students', *Australian academic and research libraries*, **19** (2), 1988, 129–39.

12

THE PUBLIC LIBRARY: THE LOCAL SUPPORT CENTRE FOR OPEN AND DISTANCE LEARNERS

Alan Watkin

Introduction

A key role for public libraries as we turn the Millennium is to provide access to and support for lifelong learning. This role is one which is valid throughout the world with local variations appropriate to local needs, traditions and patterns of library provision. Furthermore, lifelong learning will increasingly be dominated by the independent learner, the distance learner, and the open learner.

The main elements which are discussed in this chapter are:

- the role of the public library
- the key needs and requirements of open and distance learners
- EC-funded Project activity – PLAIL and LISTED Projects
- the unique features which public libraries can offer the lifelong learner.

The role of the public library

The immediate geographical and historical context of this chapter is real life experiences in the public library service in NE Wales, and in Clwyd and Wrexham in particular. In fact Clwyd as a local authority disappeared in April 1996 through a central government directed process of reorganization to create the new unitary authority of Wrexham. In the 1980s NE Wales was experiencing massive change brought about by the collapse and death of traditional industry and employment, with consequent dislocation, and equally strong social and educational change, leading to the need to develop or rediscover and redirect library provision. The particular emphasis in this context centred on three areas which were:

- services to business
- services to individuals as members of their local, democratic society
- services to lifelong learners.

The pattern of development in respect of all three elements of service share common themes, namely:

- local customer groups
- 'new' services drawing upon traditional public library resources and librarians' skills, albeit heightened or strengthened in particular respects.

A point worth emphasizing is that, in common with other chapters in this collection, this is not about any giant leap into an unknown world. It is about giving priority to certain customer groupings, and focusing and enhancing existing public library skills and resources to help meet the needs of these groups. Public library provision in this area is rooted in the founding principles of public libraries in the UK, in terms of the Victorian concept that they offered the opportunity, in the language of the period, of a source of educational development for those without the financial resources to attend more formal institutions. They were the 'poor man's university'. Certainly as centres of personal improvement they became a concept paralleled in many countries of the world, e.g. Carnegie's support for public libraries, working men's institutes etc. It is possible to see modern day comparisons to this. For example, in Portugal following the revolution of 1974, there was the need to redefine the public library's role, with the removal of closed access prohibitions and the development of new facilities to a national plan.

In Clwyd the development of provision for the lifelong learner, in practice and through controlled government sponsored research, progressed through the gradual growth of a number of interlinked elements, including:

- provision of information regarding opportunities
- development of support for the learner
- the direct delivery of learning opportunities (in particular through open and distance learning).

Adult continuing learning is of growing importance throughout Europe, as adults who seek to re-train and/or to enhance their skills and knowledge to meet the challenges of economical, technical and sociological changes, look to the distance learning method This is often from necessity in that formal institutional educational establishments may not be available locally, may not offer appropriate courses, or are not open at convenient hours such as evenings or weekends. Public libraries are ideally suited to undertake the role of providing comprehensive support services to adult independent learners including the provision of advice and guidance.

Open and distance learning

Changes in new information and communication technologies are also increasing the potential for independent learning. Increased storage capacity, processing power and more sophisticated applications are available at ever decreasing prices with the result that information technology is increasingly accessible both to end users and to non-specialist library staff. The convergence of information and communication technologies is also widening the range of potential uses.

The importance and impact of open and distance learning has been clearly recognized by the policy makers. For example, the European Commission in an official memorandum has recorded that the Commission 'is convinced that open and distance learning could play a vital role to improve access to education and training for all European citizens' in particular in:

- increasing the level of qualification of new entrants to the work force
- updating and upgrading the qualifications of the existing work force through continuing education and training
- providing training of a kind which will lead to increased rates of participation in the labour force among hitherto under-represented groups
- securing a greater synergy between education and training and economic life so as to ensure the relevance, balance and capability of application of skills and knowledge.

EC-funded projects

Beyond the immediate Welsh and UK perspective, the reorganization of customer demand and the development of appropriate responses has been furthered by European Commission-sponsored research and development projects. Two of these are described in this section.

PLAIL (Public Libraries and Adult Independent Learners)

The PLAIL Project arose out of the rapidly increasing customer demand being experienced by public librarians throughout Europe to provide information, guidance and library support material for independent learners.

Clwyd Library and Information Service led the Project, which began in January 1994 and ran until the end of 1995, with a total cost of some 334 K ecu. What the Project and the partnership clearly demonstrated was that the public library can, and does, significantly contribute to the continuous personal development of its customers.

The initial work of the PLAIL project identified the barriers which prevent access by many adults to conventional educational and training opportunities – for example, physical and logistical factors, psychological issues frequently relating to prior and bad educational experiences, family, social and work commitments and so on. Significantly the same barriers were evident in Portugal, Spain and the UK paralleling the above noted common experiences of libraries relating to increasing demand: customer need motivated by the vast and rapid economic, social and technological change in the Community.

LISTED (Library Integrated System for Telematics-based EDucation)

The LISTED Project is a twenty-seven month project which acts upon the EC Telematics for Libraries initiative by pursuing the integration of library services within distance learning. The project addresses the issue of user services based on the identification and retrieval of resources and the establishment of pilot sites for library mediated access to learning opportunities.

The major objectives of the project are:

- to review and define user needs, as outlined in this chapter
- to identify the appropriate technologies to be used and to develop procedures for the implementation of the technical solutions within the library sector
- to develop a prototype of an interactive extended catalogue software tool for use by libraries in searching and finding resources appropriate to their clients
- to create a series of pilot demonstrators of services that can be provided by libraries
- to establish and implement an evaluation procedure to ensure that the services developed during the project achieve their objectives and, where necessary, to refine and test the final amended service.

LISTED is currently striving to go live in a number of test sites – Wrexham, Solihull, Gijon, Dublin, Kildare, Setubal – in that the final software difficulties are being overcome and in each site a test, target audience has been identified to work with the project and a controlled range of data. Initially the catalogue base will have some 300–400 entries, allowing detailed and reasonably sophisticated interrogation as well as providing direct access to a very limited range of telematically delivered products. It must be remembered that LISTED is a research project and both for reasons of control and methodological validity the breadth of customers and information is being strictly contained. However a key element is that evaluation by both users and librarians is integral, and there will consequently be a two stage programme of enhancement as follows:

- during the actual project itself, with service enhancement being implemented prior to continued delivery
- following the project, in terms of a planned programme of international development as an on-going service.

Key needs and requirements of open and distance learners

The work of both the PLAIL and LISTED projects centre very much on learners who, having left the statutory education period of their life, are now intent on pursuing new or refreshed personal training and education goals. The projects also demonstrate that, because of the circumstances of the individual, this is frequently through open/distance learning processes, at least as a starting point. An outcome of the PLAIL and LISTED projects has been the identification of the needs of open and distance learners. These are for information, study materials, facilities and equipment, counselling, and support. These requirements are discussed in more detail in the following sections:

Information

Both LISTED and PLAIL concluded that it is essential that all public libraries involved with providing a service to adult independent learners should provide them with information, particularly on what sources of information on learning opportunities and facilities are available, and on the availability of courses.

Other significantly important aspects of information which should be provided include the relevance of courses to the job market, what funding is available, course fees and cost of materials, availability of suitable materials for study, information on the level of study within courses and details of any resultant qualifications.

Appropriate study materials

In the PLAIL project direct survey work with learners revealed a preference for specially-designed study packs, especially those which are written in an informal style, as the most suitable materials for adult independent learning. Books are obviously extremely important, as well as computer-based and indeed increasingly computer-delivered materials, audio and video cassettes and CD-ROMs, thus reflecting the importance and value placed upon a multimedia approach to studying. Also identified as important was the facility to retain materials for the length of an individual's study.

Adequate facilities and equipment

Suitable facilities for studying are a prerequisite in the provision of a quality service to adult independent learners. A basic need is adequate study space with an increasing emphasis as noted earlier for access to hardware/personal computers etc. The opportunity to meet other independent learners in order to discuss progress or problems, in the form of self-study groups for example, was also requested by learners as one element in helping to address the down-side of independent learning: isolation and lack of peer group contact. Another development which is of growing relevance is the use of the new technologies to facilitate communication between students, between student and tutors, and so on, whether by video-conferencing, Internet or electronic bulletin-boards.

Counselling: advice and guidance

Counselling, in the form of guidance and advice, was identified by most respondents as an essential and significant aspect of the service a public library should offer adult independent learners. The importance of this aspect of the service was reinforced by most providers. Counselling in this context includes helping adult independent learners to interpret information and assisting them to identify and assess their learning needs and goals. Assistance should also be offered to identify the level of study required.

Library staff should also identify appropriate subject areas and offer guidance to clients in the selection of appropriate courses or study material. Advice on additional learning resource needs, for example by identifying other library resources which can help the learner, will ensure that the learner makes the best possible use of the library's resources. Advice on study schedules should be offered, e.g. by helping learners to identify what pace of study is most suitable and helping them to devise a learning action plan or strategy which suits their needs and which matches the requirements of any organizations involved.

Many adult independent learners may require guidance on effective learning skills, whilst monitoring and assisting learners during their studies to give them added confidence could prove a great benefit to adult independent learners. Assisting progression by facilitating access to accreditation processes and, where appropriate, to other training or educational opportunities are also important aspects of the counselling which should be offered to adult independent learners. Although the libraries directly involved in LISTED and PLAIL gave a cautious response towards monitoring the progress of adult independent learners it should, however, be seriously considered by those authorities that are eager to provide a full and valuable service to adult independent learners. Attitudes towards assessment of progress echoed this caution, but nevertheless, there are indications that this is an increasingly important aspect of the service and it is one which has been partially recognized by colleagues in Spain and Portugal.

The research identified lack of confidence among adult independent learners and consequently providing encouragement, reassurance and positive support in order to instil confidence is one of the most valuable aspects of a personalized approach to a professional service for adult independent learners.

Unique features of public libraries

In responding to these issues it is apposite to remember some of the features, ('unique selling points') of public libraries. These include:

LOCATION   Physically based in the local community.

ACCESSIBILITY   Open at times to suit the local community and our customers.

CUSTOMER FRIENDLINESS   Considerable recent research in the UK has reinforced this point in terms of customer care and in terms that the library is viewed as a safe environment (particularly by women, members of some ethnic communities, etc.).

SUPPORT MATERIALS   The full extent of our collections.

NON-EDUCATIONAL STUDY ENVIRONMENT   Community base for the study activity which does not bring with it the sometimes unfortunate psychological baggage of a school/college environment. The study environment encapsulates the concept of both a physical space and increasingly the provision of and access to communication and IT hardware.

SUPPORT BY TRAINED STAFF   Assisted access to information and information technologies by expert staff.

Conclusion

The public library throughout Europe and beyond has an enormous potential to contribute to the learning society and community through supporting open and distance learning and learners. Public libraries frequently already undertake aspects of provision for independent learners although this is often in a rather unstructured and ad-hoc fashion. Consequently it is possible for significant service improvements to be achieved albeit that different libraries will inevitably identify appropriate elements which they could, and indeed should, provide in the short and medium term. It is through such actions that the Public Library Service can make a most significant contribution to the 'learning society'.

13

THE GENESIS PROJECT:
CUMBRIA'S LIFELONG EDUCATION PROJECT

Joe Hendry

Introduction

This lifelong learning project addresses the challenges of the next century by developing a strategy for lifelong learning, by means of distance, open and continuous learning and through the development of information technology. This Project will be a partnership between business and industry, local communities, local government, and Cumbria's education systems of colleges, schools and libraries. The philosophy central to the Genesis Project is to build a relationship with the people of the County of Cumbria in the UK such that it creates a sense of identity with local people, and enhances people's lives. Because of Cumbria's particular circumstances it is especially well placed to develop this Project. It is unfettered by many of the academic traditions of the past. Therefore, it has a special opportunity to develop a process of lifelong learning, including higher education, that will be pivotal in providing a new kind of learning in society. Its significance will be international and community based. Genesis will place Cumbria in the vanguard of the dramatic economic, social and cultural changes which the new millennium heralds, and which will impact on all of developed society, in the UK, in Europe, and throughout the world.

This chapter outlines the background and context for the Genesis Project and the Project's objectives, and summarizes the results of a MORI survey which profiled the local community in Cumbria and identified their requirements in planning for the Project.

Context

The Genesis Project is a visionary, community based, lifelong learning process. It adopts a holistic approach to the educational, economic and social needs of Cumbria. In UK terms Cumbria is geographically very isolated. Long distances separate its communities and over 40% of its population lives in settlements of fewer than 10,000 people. Many of these communities face severe disadvantages, as the normal facilities, expected as part of life in the last years of the twentieth century, are available only in the larger towns, which are often a considerable distance away.

Its economy is dominated by high and medium level technology manufacturing, especially on the west Cumbria coast. This is complemented by tourism, which provides relatively lowly paid jobs to a predominantly female workforce in the rural setting of the Lake District. Much of the west coast's economy suffers from a legacy of industrial dereliction and poor infrastructure, which hampers attempts to foster economic development. Elsewhere in Cumbria the rural economy is under threat, with perhaps 4,000 jobs likely to disappear from agriculture during the remainder of the 1990s.

Cumbria faces major challenges in maintaining its ways of life and traditions. In no area of Cumbrian life is this more apparent than in the field of education. There are a large number of small primary schools with limited teaching resources and which have difficulty in covering the full range of the national curriculum. In secondary education, in many areas, it is not possible to provide a full range of subjects to give Cumbria's young people real opportunities for their future. Many rural secondary schools have no sixth form, and therefore no opportunity for their pupils to obtain A-levels, other than by transferring to other, more distant, secondary schools. Young people need A-levels in order to secure a university place, and higher education developments remain very limited. Further education faces difficulties with numbers of students often insufficient to justify commercially the range of courses wanted by local people.

Similar problems exist in the provision of related public services. Traditional and conventional solutions will not provide these opportunities in Cumbria. Nor does Cumbria have the critical mass of population and population density to make it commercially viable for the international telecommunications industry to invest in an electronic communications infrastructure, such as a comprehensive broadband network, to allow Cumbria's industries, education services and communities to be able to participate in the evolving information society of the next millennium.

Cumbria now needs a solution to these disadvantages by developing a new, community based method of providing lifelong education at every level. The Genesis Project will prepare Cumbria, its people and its industries for the challenges of the twenty-first century and beyond.

The Genesis Project

The Genesis Projects aims to change and improve Cumbria's circumstances through the following solutions.

1   Link local schools together across Cumbria, thus improving the quality of education and the ability to teach in new and innovative ways.

2   Network all existing colleges of further and higher education and go on to link these with Cumbria's local schools, thus providing access to educational opportunities at every level, irrespective of the location of the academic institution or school.

3   Enable all public sector agencies to share and disseminate information so that a service can be provided effectively to all communities in a way that is not possible at present. A direct result will be that Cumbrians will have greatly improved information about services available to them. They will have the ability to have their questions answered and their problems dealt with, without leaving their local area.

4   Network existing services to business and commerce to provide better and more readily accessible information and advice. This will assist these businesses to develop and thus provide enhanced job opportunities. This process would allow businesses to access advice and support not only from public agencies such as the Training and Enterprise Council and Business Link, but from the resources of further and higher education throughout Cumbria.

5   Provide the means to develop new opportunities for higher education delivered on a distance learning basis from existing university outlets within Cumbria, new outlets developed as a result of the Project, and from academic institutions outside Cumbria, whether in other parts of the UK or elsewhere in the world.

6   Create an opportunity for Cumbria's tourist industry to provide a network of information throughout Cumbria, and which can then be accessed world-wide via the Internet. This information would relate to accommodation, attractions, amenities, other places to visit and their accessibility. It would thus allow immediate electronic booking facilities in a way equivalent to that currently used by the international travel industry.

7   Deliver a digital library facility which would, initially, provide access to all books and publications in all the institutions forming part of the network. Eventually, technological advance would also create a paperless library with access to information being gained through electronic means.

8   Offer commercial opportunities to sell capacity on the network to businesses wishing to promote their products within and beyond Cumbria. This would provide on-going finance to ensure the long-term viability of the network. It would also establish an international electronic commerce facility for small and medium sized Cumbrian enterprises to compete in international markets.

9   Utilize schools, colleges, libraries and village halls as community facilities for continuous learning in a way that, at present, is simply not available.

The Genesis Project will therefore be realized by the development of the process of lifelong learning, under-pinned by the incremental development of an advanced, broadband electronic communication and IT infrastructure which will support those economic, educational, public and social goals in a combined, seamless manner. Such an infrastructure will not only secure the effective regeneration of Cumbria's economy, dramatically improve its educational opportunities, and provide coordination and access to public services, it will encourage partnership and collaboration, enhance external communication, and allow the rural and urban economies and community life to flourish, by permitting Cumbria to communicate simply and effectively in itself, and with the rest of the world.

While the information revolution has the potential to bring remarkable benefits, it also has the capacity to widen dramatically the gap between the information rich and the information poor: in local communities, within nations, and between the developed and the developing world. In Cumbria at least, there is a determination that this will not happen.

Planning for the Project

To provide a sound basis for planning the Genesis Project, a substantial survey of local opinion has been commissioned. The household survey was undertaken by the market research organization MORI. Other aspects of the research were supervised by the Market Research Society (MRS).

The market research had four specific aims:

- to establish current access to IT and information services, including sources and technologies used now (e.g. access to the Internet) and current IT skill levels
- to establish attitudes to informal learning and the potential for using IT in this way
- to identify currently existing barriers to utilization of information and take up of learning opportunities
- to establish users needs and preferences for accessing information technology (for example how far individuals would travel to use IT resources, how much individuals would pay for specialist services).

The household survey undertaken by MORI allowed reliable estimates to be made about attitudes and experience of individuals of different ages and social classes. Since the survey should take into account the views of individuals living in all parts of Cumbria, the sample included a cross-section of those living in towns, villages, and those in more remote locations. MORI surveyed 1500 individuals.

There was overwhelming support for the Genesis Project, with more than half of those surveyed 'strongly supporting' and a further third 'tending to support'. Of those with an opinion, only 2% 'tended to oppose' the aims of Genesis, and no one opposed the project strongly. This shows something of the latent potential and enthusiasm waiting to be tapped.

Nine out of every ten people interviewed felt that they would be likely to use the services offered. There was a clear appreciation of:

- more limited job opportunities and the problems in finding out about these opportunities
- the remoteness, poorer transport links and consequent difficulty in travelling to services
- there being less for young people to do
- the high quality of the environment.

In each of these areas the Genesis Project will deliver significant benefits to Cumbrians.

In terms of how well informed people felt about local services and facilities, about a third of the population felt ill informed. However those who felt well informed were more likely to use Genesis to improve existing knowledge.

Although nearly everyone had heard of most technologies, usage was much more limited. A quarter of people would like to use the Internet, CD-ROMs and the World Wide Web but cannot because of issues associated with cost and access to equipment. At present two-thirds or more of the population do not wish to use e-mail, the Internet, mobile phones, the World Wide Web, fax or telephone banking. These tend to be people who are currently information disempowered. Genesis will empower this section of the community by making current information resources accessible to many who would otherwise be excluded from the emerging information society.

People surveyed, and the analysis of their reactions, could be categorized as being of three types: 'enthusiasts and acceptors', 'concerned and unconvinced' and the 'alienated'.

Enthusiasts and acceptors

Nationally 25% of the population are adept and comfortable with both the idea and the reality of technology. Generally this group think that computers are a good idea and want to learn more. This group tends to be younger people, often men, and in higher socio-economic groups. In Cumbria about 40% felt confident about computers. Nearly half of these had experienced e-mail and computers at work. However access to technology and skills was a problem for this group. They were very enthusiastic about Genesis and the power it would offer them and their communities.

Concerned and unconvinced

Generally, this group has mixed feelings about the effects of computerization on society, but are keen to learn more. The group makes up around one in five of the population and comprises many older people, typically men who are over 45 and C2DE women of all ages. These groups are also concerned that they will not be able to learn. This a key group for the Genesis Project. In Cumbria this group comprises about 25% of the population. They are positive about the benefits of Genesis and would like to use the Internet and CD-ROM. Price, availability and training were the key limiters of use outside the work environment.

The alienated

This group is likely to be the most resistant to the onset of the information society. They are typically C2DE women aged 55+. When asked about computer technology the group said 'don't use and don't want to use'. This group was the least confident about computers but significantly fewer were resistant to using computers to get community information, particularly if access was local and free of charge. The MORI survey reinforced the results of the demonstrations: when shown a relevant application this group changed their opinion. When asked about Genesis very few of the group opposed the project and most said they would like to use information about local news, events and services.

National research carried out in the UK by Motorola has pointed to the development of a nation of IT 'haves' and 'have nots' which mirror existing social divides. Although the MORI work in Cumbria has confirmed this danger it has also pointed to an enthusiasm to avoid the dangers of disempowerment and to make use of services being offered through Genesis.

Services people most wished to access included local news and events (three-quarters supported); community advice (two-thirds supported) and public transport information (a half supported). Training, jobs, childcare and disability information had niche audiences. A great diversity in community information requirements is beginning to emerge. The Genesis approach offers an opportunity to serve all of these niche markets. Most favoured local sites for Genesis were libraries and schools (half each). Village halls/community centres were also popular potential locations.

Although many people were confident that they could make good use of emerging technologies, and wished to learn more about their potential, the cost of the equipment purchase is currently restricting access significantly. For example amongst children, the group with greatest exposure to IT, only around a third have experience of the Internet.

Amongst the whole population, nationally 13% have experienced the Internet: in Cumbria only 7%. However four times this number would like to use the Internet. This emphasizes Cumbria's relatively weak current position but a strong demand for access and training. The single issue which people felt would encourage more use of these technologies was local training and advice, free of charge.

Conclusion

The Genesis programme identifies a range of business, community and lifelong learning services which it is anticipated will be used by the citizens of Cumbria. The services were included from experience gained by public demand in a range of agencies including libraries, information centres, council offices, Business Links, schools, colleges and the TEC. We have been able to gauge needs further by use of the MORI Household Survey and the Genesis Road Show. Results from both of these have confirmed that our original proposals were accurate, with a potentially significant take-up of each type of service offered.

Whilst the MORI Household Survey enabled people to consider a wide range of issues concerning IT and information services, the Genesis Road Show enabled direct public access to a wide range of information and learning services using different IT devices including touch-screen access and video-conferencing. This confirmation that our proposed services are in demand led us to draw up a schedule of our planned Phase I Implementation Strategy. This will consist of 140 access points on 20 sites throughout Cumbria. It will include eight public access touch screen terminals in partnership with British Telecom and will be launched in January 1998.

In summary, Genesis aims to:

- educate, train and re-skill people
- establish new, knowledge based industries
- attract high technology inward investment
- maintain the social quality of our local communities while linking them together, and with the outside world
- provide a vastly improved telecommunications infrastructure to enable existing industry and commerce to compete effectively with the rest of the world
- support the existing internationally recognized Cumbrian research establishments

- encourage the formation and development of further research facilities and their links with industry.

Genesis has the potential to become the flagship for Cumbria's educational and cultural industries, and to establish knowledge-based industries as a major employer and wealth creator in the next century.

14

THE UNIVERSE PROJECT:
GLOBAL, DISTRIBUTED LIBRARY SERVICES

Ian Pettman and Suzanne Ward

Introduction

UNIverse is a large scale project based on the concept of a virtual union catalogue for libraries, making distributed information resources accessible for searching, retrieving, requesting and delivery in an integrated environment. The Project is funded under the European Commission's Libraries Programme. The Consortium combines some of Europe's leading developers of networked information systems with influential practitioners from the world of academic and national libraries.

In order to deliver this vision of integrated services, the Project will apply open standards and protocols. In addition to these, further technical issues surrounding service distribution and globalization currently facing information service providers and users will also be addressed, such as deduplicating multiple records, handling different record structures (via UNIMARC) and languages (via Unicode) within one system.

From a management perspective UNIverse is raising issues concerning the provision of mediated versus non-mediated information services. The technology will enable librarians to empower their end users to access remote sources without recourse to their home library. The results of a survey undertaken by the project of end users and librarians indicate, however, that the main counter argument to 'user empowerment' is the 'problem' for the library of verifying requests and managing payment.

The UNIverse system will undergo extensive evaluation with users from June 1998 to March 1999. Two types of user communities are being set up. The first is focused around the national library partners in the Project. The second will be subject based groups in environmental and technical sciences. Both groups represent very dispersed user communities, where service delivery frequently takes place remotely either across technical networks or using traditional (print based) delivery methods.

This chapter represents the library's or information provider's perspective, looking at how to meet the changing needs of end users, be they scholars or members of the public, within the existing framework of libraries and information providers.

This chapter will show how UNIverse is addressing the technical and management issues facing all of us. It starts with an overview of UNIverse, clarifying the aims and objectives, before moving on to describe the rationale and the background to the Project. It will also look briefly at how the software will be put together and then move on to how to assess whether it meets librarians' and users' needs, which are considered the most important issues.

A more detailed description of the origins and evolution of the project is given in Murray and Pettman.[1] Descriptions of the underpinning standards, softwares and systems are given in Clissman et al.[2-4]

What is UNIverse?

The full title of the UNIverse Project is 'Large scale demonstrators for global open distributed library systems'. It is one of the proposals selected by the European Commission for support under the 4th Framework Telematics for Libraries Programme. It is intended that the project should run for 30 months from October 1996 to March 1999. The total cost of the Project will be in the region of four million ecus.

The Consortium consists of six full partners and 11 associate partners (Table 14.1). Provision is also made for a large user group (around 50 libraries directly participating in project trials). The full partners are from four EU member states

Table 14.1 *Consortium partners*

Full partners	Associate partners
British Library	Ex-Libris
Danish Technical Knowledge Centre	Forbairt
Freshwater Biological Association	Harper Adams College
Fretwell-Downing Informatics Ltd	Southampton Oceanography Centre
Irish Library Council	Index Data
National Library of Greece	Kyros
	Q-Ray
	University College Dublin
	Technical University of Delft
	Norwegian Technical University
	University of Sheffield library

(Denmark, GB, Greece and Ireland) whilst the associate partners span seven states (Holland, Luxembourg and Norway, in addition to the above). It is anticipated that the active user group participants will further broaden geographic participation within the community.

The 17 organizations involved in the consortium present a balance between libraries of various categories and small to medium size enterprises (SMEs). Of the 12 libraries, three are national libraries, seven are specialist subject libraries (relating to the subject area demonstrators proposed) whilst two are broad based academic libraries.The five commercial organizations are all SMEs: four are suppliers of library automation and the fifth provides consultancy services in the fields of high technology. Out of the 17 members seven are new to the Framework Programme, whilst the others have all participated in the 3rd Framework Libraries Programme as well as a number of other relevant RTD initiatives.

The partner responsible for coordinating impact assessment and validation will be the Information Studies Department of the University of Sheffield. This Department has an international reputation for action research in the information community and for its contribution to the training of librarians.

What is UNIverse about ?

UNIverse is about overcoming some of the major current limitations in libraries, such as:

- other finding tools being more 'user friendly' than library catalogues, leading to under use of these excellent search sources
- physically distributed catalogues and databases causing the user more inconvenience and difficulty
- managing searching over multiple catalogues (problems relating to differing record formats, duplicate records, speed of response, foreign language search terms etc.)
- disjointed services from searching to delivery – in most existing systems, the search system and interface is separate from the request system and interface.

UNIverse is also about modernizing library services in order to:

- meet changes in education (student-centred/independent/distance learning)
- meet changes in user expectations of how information technology will help them find information in a range of formats.

The Project therefore has three main objectives, which are to:

- produce innovative software making distributed library catalogues into an efficient and effective virtual union catalogue
- produce innovative software integrating services around the virtual union catalogue
- provide demonstrator services to show that the system is practical and to evaluate its ability to meet present and future requirements.

Systems operation

The large number of geographically distributed library catalogues, which under the UNIverse project will behave as a virtual union catalogue, should deliver a number of high quality library services to both the end user and the librarian. These are:

- search and retrieve – very large scale, transparent multi-database searching
- multimedia document delivery – integrated to the search and retrieve process
- interlibrary loans – integrated to the search and retrieve process
- collaborative cataloguing/record supply – an efficiency gain for the librarian.

Technical perspective

First we will consider the operation of such a system from the technical perspective. The key features of the UNIverse architecture for the virtual union catalogue include:

- the ability to search in parallel, multiple physical databases which have a variety of access methods, record syntax, character sets and languages, presenting the results as if a single logical database were being searched
- the multiplicity of data sources hidden from the user and a high quality of service achieved both in terms of performance and data quality through record de-duplication and merging
- the use of open distributed processing techniques through which the architecture has potentially unlimited scalability whilst maintaining high performance.

To achieve this functionality UNIverse is building on the outcomes of three previous EC Framework projects: IRIS, one of the first Z39.50-based distributed catalogues offering document delivery, single hit-list, and e-mail requesting; EUROPAGATE, a Z39.50 and ISO SR IR gateway with MARC data conversion as an additional service; and DALI, which is IRIS plus online multimedia document delivery.

The Project is committed to the use, exploitation and further development of standards in every aspect of the system and is reliant on them to achieve its objectives. In particular, we are using standards for searching/retrieving (ISO239.50), requesting (ISO ILL), identifying the format of electronic documents (GEDI), record formats (UNIMARC) and record syntax/character sets (Unicode).

The identification, de-duplication and manipulation of serial items will be essential elements of the system. The project will also therefore be working with USBC (the Universal Standard Bibliographic Code), SICI (the Serial Item and Contribution Identifier) which is defined in ANSI/NISO Z39.50 – 199X, and DOI (the Digital Object Identifiers) systems.

System architecture

Starting at the top of Figure 14.1, there will be three possible forms of access to the system. The specific UNIverse Client being developed by the Project will obviously give the highest level of functionality. It will, however, be possible for users to access the system using their own Z39.50 client or a Java-enabled WWW client.

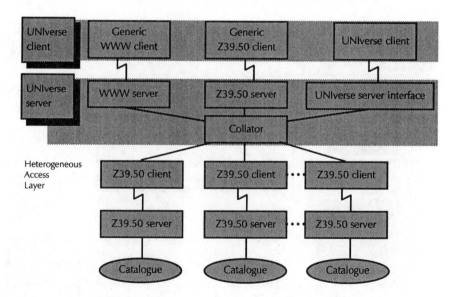

Fig. 14.1 Diagrammatic overview of the system architecture based on a client–server approach

Search requests from these clients will then pass through a UNIverse server (central block of the diagram) to the remote targets (Heterogeneous Access Layer of the diagram). These remote targets may all be individual library catalogues. However, any of these could be another UNIverse server thus enabling unlimited scalability of the system. These databases will be searched simultaneously, not serially, in order to improve response time.

The simplified schematic diagram (Figure 14.2) gives some indication of the operations required within this software package.

The central component of the UNIverse server is the collator. It interacts with a number of modules that produce enhancements to the software, such as:

- Character set conversion – where records coming into the server in different character sets are converted to the format requested by the client interface.
- Record conversion – where records coming into the server in different formats are converted to the format requested by the client interface.
- Language conversion – before issuing a search, the search term may be checked against a multilingual thesaurus for translation before it is issued to the target databases.
- Profile database – will hold information about target databases concerning content and database capability.
- Query adaptation – by knowing about the capabilities of the target servers, the

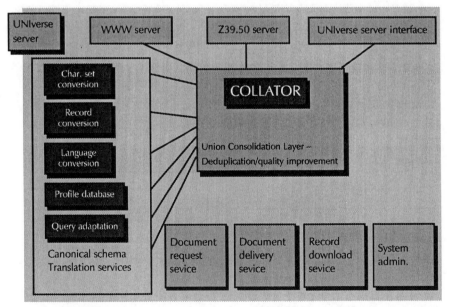

Fig. 14.2 *UNIverse system components*

UNIverse server can adapt queries to fit the target.

The collator also carries out the de-duplication process/quality improvement, whereby hits will be de-duplicated according to defined algorithms (some under user control) and the resulting records enhanced. These are the essential technical building blocks of the system. UNIverse, however, is about end-user services and exactly how these blocks are specified and put together depends on the user requirements.

User perspective

UNIverse is very much about modernizing library services in order to give:

- remote access to (remote) information sources
- remote delivery of (remote) information
- services which the end-user can use without having to refer to the librarian
- seamless integrated services.

Figure 14.3 illustrates the four core services available in UNIverse, which are: searching/retrieving; requesting/inter library loan; document delivery; record supply/collaborative cataloguing. The system should be relevant to both end users

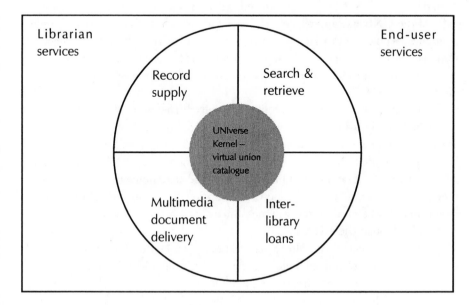

Fig. 14.3 UNIverse core services

and librarians, although record supply is likely only to be of interest to librarians.

Consultation with users

UNIverse is a user oriented project and we are consulting widely with librarians and end users. Consultation will take two forms, a general survey of requirements (which has already been undertaken) and the setting up of Special Interest Groups (SIGs) of libraries to both demonstrate and evaluate the software.

The general survey of requirements (undertaken during February/March 1997) was designed to give data on how competent potential users were with computers and what they thought about the type of services that were being proposed through UNIverse. The results have enabled a general user profile to be constructed for the evaluation phase. The majority of users will:

- come from the academic/research community
- have IT experience
- want access to information resources from both within the library and from their desktop.

Librarians' responses

Librarians were asked specifically to comment on what they thought the advantages of the UNIverse approach were. They felt that it would increase user independence, would mean that users would not have to visit the library to access resources and would increase the range of bibliographic services available to users. It might also save users' time and, in effect it would be a one-stop shop for their information needs.

Their concerns about the UNIverse approach centred on how competent their users would be in using the system. This has a particular knock-on effect on the amount of training that would need to be given. They were also concerned as to how librarians would be able to control budgets when end users no longer needed to go through librarians to submit requests and take delivery of items. It was thought that this might be too expensive an option. They also thought that users might be overwhelmed by the volume of material which would be available and accessible through the system.

Librarians' concerns have already been anticipated by the Project partners and a systems administration module will be available on the UNIverse server to accommodate these concerns. In this module librarians will be able to set the parameters within which they want the UNIverse service to operate within their organization. For example: user profiles can be defined to categorize type of user and level of access to resources; users can be given authorization to access services and to order documents; all use can be tracked and all transactions logged, for the purposes of copyright tracking and/or payment.

The evaluation

The final nine month phase of the Project (July 1998 to March 1999), as well as testing and correcting the software, will be a major evaluation exercise. It is envisaged that 60 libraries will be involved in this phase (six from the partners and an extra 54 in the user groups). They will be organized into Special Interest Groups (SIGs) (Figure 14.4) in order to demonstrate, test and evaluate the software in a working environment.

The three national libraries will contribute high volume data sets and it is anticipated that their involvement will have a catalytic effect in broadening the uptake of the system. The pan-European catalogues in technology and environmental sciences are intended to stimulate cross border cooperation and resource sharing. The two library software systems user groups will represent the requirements of the libraries using the software from the two major library systems suppliers involved in the development of UNIverse.

The User Group coordinators are Technical University of Delft (Technical

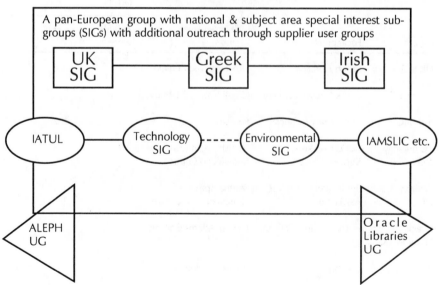

Fig. 14.4 *The special interest groups*

SIG), Freshwater Biological Association (Environmental SIG) and Irish Library Council, National Library of Greece and The British Library (National SIGs).

Each SIG coordinator is responsible for the recruitment of a certain number of database providers (via Z39.50 servers) and libraries willing to use the UNIverse clients in each SIG (Table 14.2).

Progess to date
Phase one – October 1996 to June 1997

During this phase the Project infrastructure was established and a Project handbook was produced. This standard procedure is even more essential than normal in a project of this size and complexity. Two state of the art assessment reports have been produced: 'Technical state of the art' and 'User services state of the art'.

A range of requirements analyses documents have been produced. These are:

* a technical requirements specification including profile requirements, document formats and transport mechanisms

Table 14.2 *The provisional distribution of the SIGs*

Aspect	Focal point	UNIverse server location	Active libraries targets	
			Z39.50 servers	Clients
UK SIG	British Library	University of Sheffield	4	6
Greek SIG	Greek National Library	Greek National Library	2	2
Irish SIG	Irish Library Council	Forbairt	6	7
Technology SIG	Danish Technical Knowledge Centre	Danish Technical Knowledge Centre	4	5
Environmental SIG	Freshwater Biological Association	Southampton Oceanography Centre	2	3
Oracle Libraries UG	Harper Adams College	Harper Adams College	3	4
ALEPH UG	Ex-Libris	To be decided	3	3
Overall	Irish Library Council		24	30

- project critical success factors
- user requirements specification for search and retrieve, document requesting/ILL, document delivery and collaborative cataloguing
- service scenarios including legal and commercial requirements.

Phase two – July 1997 to June 1998

The two main areas of work during this period will be:

- system design build and test
- user group development.

At the time of writing (September 1997) the following has been achieved. For the design, specification and selection of software, 18 areas have been identified under this sector and reports prepared for them. The software build is underway, and integration has been scheduled for December 1997 to March 1998. The alpha test will take place April 1998 to June 1998.

For user group development, letters of invitation to participate, detailed descriptions of the Project for potential participants and draft contracts are nearing completion. A service manual is in preparation and user group meetings are being scheduled and planned.

Phase three – July 1998 to March 1999

The work in this phase involves demonstrator service establishment and operation, impact assessment, validation and future implementation and exploitation plans.

Underpinning all three phases is a concerted research, liaison and dissemination work package. The UNIverse research raises some important issues for the successful delivery of a true global information infrastructure, for example, natural language processing for multilingual queries, optimal methods for searching massive parallel databases, expert systems for record de-duplication etc. UNIverse intends to liaise with research projects in these areas and contribute to them.

The Project progress and results will be disseminated through publications and presentation at workshops and conferences. There is liaison with related EC Libraries Programme projects (e.g. EUROPAGATE, IRIS, DALI, ARCA, G7 etc.), and also with all relevant standards bodies and interest groups (e.g. EFILA, ZIG, PIG etc.). Since standards are constantly being revised it is necessary to monitor the progress of these groups to ensure that the Project is current. It is also intended to make the Project results available to the standards bodies, particularly in relation to inter-operability and possible extensions to support enhanced functionality.

Further information on the UNIverse Project

For further information on the UNIverse project contact:

George Bingham (UNIverse Project Manager)
Fretwell Downing Data Systems Ltd
Brincliffe House
861 Ecclesall Road
SHEFFIELD S11 7AE
UK
E-mail: gbingham@fdgroup.co.uk
URL: <http://www.fdgroup.co.uk/research/universe>

References

1   Murray, R. and Pettman, I., 'The UNIverse project' *New library world*, **98** (1133), 1997, 53–9.

2   Clissman, C., et al., 'The UNIverse project: state of the art of the standards, softwares and systems which will underpin the development. Part 1: Z39.50; WWW Integration with Z39.50; and Unicode', *New library world*, **98**, (1138), 1997, 267–74.

3   Clissman, C., et al., 'The UNIverse project: state of the art of the standards, softwares and systems which will underpin the development. Part 2: record syntax conversion, result set de-duplication and multilingual thesauri', *New library world*, **99** (1139), 1998, 10–19.

4   Clissman, C., et al., 'The UNIverse project: state of the art of the standards, softwares and systems which will underpin the development. Part 3: Inter Library Loan and Multi-Media Document Delivery', *New library world*, **99** (1140), 1998 (in press).

Index